SENSE & NONSENSE
ABOUT
HEAVEN
& HELL

SENSE & NONSENSE
ABOUT
HEAVEN
& HELL

KENNETH D. BOA
ROBERT M. BOWMAN JR.

ZONDERVAN®

ZONDERVAN.com/
AUTHORTRACKER
follow your favorite authors

Sense and Nonsense about Heaven and Hell
Copyright © 2007 by Kenneth D. Boa and Robert M. Bowman Jr.

Requests for information should be addressed to:

Zondervan, *Grand Rapids, Michigan* 49530

Library of Congress Cataloging-in-Publication Data

Boa, Kenneth.
    Sense and nonsense about heaven and hell / Kenneth Boa and Robert M.
Bowman Jr.
      p. cm.
    Includes bibliographical references and index.
    ISBN-13: 978-0-310-25428-7
    ISBN-10: 0-310-25428-0
    1. Heaven. 2. Hell. 3. Future life. I. Bowman, Robert M. II. Title.
BT846.3.B63 2007
236'.24 — dc22

2007001535

Published in association with the literary agency of Wolgemuth & Associates, Inc.

Interior design by Mark Sheeres

Printed in the United States of America

07 08 09 10 11 12 • 15 14 13 12 11 10 9 8 7 6 5 4 3 2

CONTENTS

ABBREVIATIONS

AB   Anchor Bible
ACCS   Ancient Christian Commentary on Scripture
AnBib   Analecta biblica
BECNT   Baker Exegetical Commentary on the New Testament
BETS   *Bulletin of the Evangelical Theological Society*
BSac   *Bibliotheca Sacra*
BT   *Bible Translator*
ESV   English Standard Version
HCSB   Holman Christian Standard Bible
JETS   *Journal of the Evangelical Theological Society*
KJV   King James Version
LCC   Library of Christian Classics
NASB   New American Standard Bible
NCBC   New Century Bible Commentary
NET   New English Translation (NET Bible)
NICNT   New International Commentary on the New Testament
NIGTC   New International Greek Testament Commentary
NIV   New International Version
NKJV   New King James Version
NovT   *Novum Testamentum*
NRSV   New Revised Standard Version
NWT   New World Translation
TrinJ   *Trinity Journal*
WBC   Word Biblical Commentary
WTJ   *Westminster Theological Journal*

PREFACE

Heaven may be one of the safest subjects on which anyone could write. No one on Earth knows exactly what Heaven will be like, but almost everyone agrees that it will be wonderful. So, just say nice things about Heaven and you're home free. On the other hand, it's easy to offend people when talking about Hell. After all, the very idea of a Hell is offensive to many people. What's even more offensive is the suggestion that some people might actually *go* there.

We have no desire to offend anyone unnecessarily. However, in this book we're not going to hold back from saying things that might offend people. Regrettably, a lot of what is said today about both Heaven and Hell is nonsense. False, sometimes absurd ideas about what happens after we die confuse millions. Bestselling books offer testimonies from apparently sincere, earnest individuals reporting that they visited Heaven — or occasionally Hell — and can tell us exactly what it is like.

Our goal in this book is to help you think clearly and critically about the subject of Heaven and Hell. To that end, we look at a variety of beliefs about this subject. Although we are Christians, we identify some nonsense coming from Christian as well as non-Christian sources. In that respect, we are "equal-opportunity offenders": we think nonsense should be exposed wherever it may be found, even in our own religious backyard.

The focus of this book will be on getting a clearheaded understanding of what the Bible says on this subject. We refute common misconceptions about Heaven and Hell in order to foster a biblically sound view of death and eternity. We warn about the dangers of false teachings on the afterlife prevalent in our society. In so doing, we clarify fundamental truths about God and his purpose for our lives.

One minor detail: We capitalize *Heaven* and *Hell* when those words refer to the final disposition of the redeemed and the unredeemed. We do not capitalize them when used in other ways (e.g., "heaven" may refer to the sky; "hell" may refer to the abode of the dead awaiting judgment).

Without further ado, then, let's start sorting out sense and nonsense about Heaven and Hell.

Chapter 1

THE MAKE-YOUR-OWN-HEAVEN GAME

There are lots of different ideas about Heaven, and some of them must be wrong.

If human beings were created for an eternal existence, nothing could be more important than finding out what that eternal future is all about and making sure that we are going in the right direction. Yet we find ourselves today confronted with a broad spectrum of beliefs about Heaven and Hell. In this chapter, we will concentrate on the diverse views regarding Heaven.

Of course, some people don't believe in Heaven at all. To them we ask one simple question: Do you believe in God? If you do, then it shouldn't be too tough to believe in Heaven. If you don't believe in God, nothing we can say about Heaven will make much sense to you. The question of God's existence is *logically prior* to the question of Heaven's existence. So we encourage those who don't yet believe in God, or are unsure about God's existence, to examine the evidence on that subject before tackling the issue of Heaven.[1]

BLAISE PASCAL

All our actions and thoughts must take such different courses, according as there are or are not eternal joys to hope for, that it is impossible to take one step with sense and judgment unless we regulate our course by our view of this point which ought to be our ultimate end.[2]

Modern and Postmodern Heavens

The history of modern views of Heaven begins with Emanuel Swedenborg (1688–1772). Swedenborg was a brilliant if eccentric thinker who distinguished himself in the sciences but left his most influential (and controversial) mark in religion. Many of the features of Swedenborg's theological system have made their way into the views of Heaven in modern cults as well as the broad range of Western (especially American) pop culture:

- Angels are human beings who have died and become perfect.
- There are "three heavens" corresponding to varying degrees of closeness to God.
- The highest of those three heavens has specific features matched or duplicated in the physical world (such as having an east, west, north, and south).
- People of all religions will go to Heaven.
- We can learn a lot about Heaven from modern reports of personal visits to or from Heaven.

The last of these features has been especially important for modern beliefs about Heaven. Swedenborg himself claims to have had lengthy discussions with angels about both Heaven and Hell:

> ... it has been granted me to associate with angels and to talk with them as man with man, also to see what is in the heavens and what is in the hells, and this for thirteen years; so now from what I have seen and heard it has been granted me to describe these, in the hope that ignorance may thus be enlightened and unbelief dissipated.[3]

Modern writers have often produced extremely detailed descriptions of the spirit realm. In recent years we have seen a spate of books telling about the authors' visits to Heaven, such as Betty Eadie's *Embraced by the Light*.[4]

In the nineteenth century, new religions combined some of the above elements of Swedenborg's visions of Heaven (whether they got them directly from him or not) with more traditional Christian elements. The Church of Jesus Christ of Latter-day Saints (Mormons) teaches that people existed in Heaven as spirit children of

God the Father and were sent to Earth as a testing ground. Most people, according to Mormonism, will end up in one of three heavens, with only faithful Mormons (along with those who convert in the spirit world and prove their worthiness there) returning to live with God in the highest, "celestial" Heaven.

Jehovah's Witnesses teach that only 144,000 "anointed" Christians will go to Heaven as spirit beings of the same nature as angels. Most of the members of this "anointed class" will be either first-century believers or Jehovah's Witnesses baptized before 1935. Most of the rest of humanity (the "other sheep") will live on Earth during the Millennium and then, if they prove themselves worthy, will live forever as perfected human beings on a Paradise Earth. Like another religion to emerge in the nineteenth century, the Seventh-day Adventist Church (and numerous other Adventist groups), Jehovah's Witnesses deny that the wicked will suffer unending punishment. They claim that the Hell of the Bible is actually the grave and that when people die, they cease to exist.

Another group of religions to emerge in the nineteenth century were the mind sciences, which include Unity, New Thought, and Christian Science. The mind sciences view Heaven as the unseen present dimension or presence of the divine Mind in all things, accessible to anyone who has learned to think properly. Mary Baker Eddy, the founder of Christian Science, defined Heaven as follows: "Harmony; the reign of Spirit; government spirituality; bliss; the atmosphere of Soul." She explained, "Heaven is not a locality, but a divine state of Mind in which all the manifestations of Mind are harmonious and immortal."[5]

This does not mean that the mind sciences deny life after death, except insofar as some of them deny the reality of death! Rather, most

ANTHONY DESTEFANO

In the case of heaven, the "old news" of traditional Christianity is infinitely more exciting, interesting, uplifting, and fun that anything expounded by TV psychics or "new age" gurus.[6]

advocates of the mind sciences believe that our minds or spirits will continue to progress after the death of our bodies (or what appears to be death) and experience Heaven in a more complete way.

Similar views are also found in the New Age movement, which in significant ways is an outgrowth of the mind sciences. One interesting difference is that many New Agers believe in reincarnation. The idea of reincarnation was imported into Western society from Hindu and Buddhist religious traditions in Asia and reinterpreted to fit Western scientific thinking and cultural sensibilities. Reincarnation functions in New Age thought as an alternate explanation of how human spirits can perfect themselves and so attain to Heaven.

In the second half of the twentieth century, numerous small cults reinterpreted elements of traditional religion (usually Christianity) as references to earthly interaction with UFOs. For these cults, UFOs bring messages from Heaven, which may be viewed as outer space or a particular planet, or as an extradimensional realm.[7]

Heaven: The Extremes

We find it helpful to think about these diverse views of Heaven as fitting onto a spectrum. At one extreme end of the spectrum are completely spiritualized notions of Heaven, such as the mind science belief that Heaven is the harmony or inner perfection of our present existence. Those who take this extreme position don't think of Heaven as a reality distinct from our physical world. To them, Heaven is here and now, if we have the faith or mindset to believe it.

At the other end of the spectrum are materialized notions of Heaven. For example, some people believe that Heaven is another planet or some other physical location in outer space. As we have just noted, UFO cults typically take this view. Ironically, these thoroughly materialistic views of Heaven also don't think of it as a distinct reality. In other words, both extremely spiritualized and extremely materialistic views of Heaven view it as indistinguishable from physical reality.

Between these two extremes lie more familiar beliefs. Toward the spiritualized end, but not so extreme, is the belief that in Heaven all human beings will live forever in the form of angels or angel-like spirits with no physical bodies. Toward the materialized end, but again not so extreme, is the view that Heaven is a literal location with physical properties and will feature a city with literal streets of gold.

Colleen McDannell and Bernhard Lang, in their influential book *Heaven: A History*, propose another useful way to categorize different views of Heaven. They classify views of Heaven into those that are "theocentric" (God-centered) or "God-oriented," and those that are "anthropocentric" (man-centered), or "people-oriented." A theocentric view of Heaven understands eternal life as exclusively, or at least primarily, consisting of an immediate experience of God. An anthropocentric view of Heaven understands it as consisting primarily of unspoiled relationships with other creatures, especially one's family and friends.

McDannell and Lang characterize the theocentric view of Heaven as that typical of religious enthusiasts (among whom they include Jesus) and "naïve" intellectuals, with the anthropocentric view being the more prevalent and natural view of common people. "For all its sophistication and brilliant argumentation, theological intellectualism with its insistence on a God-centered hereafter has never been able to erase the natural longing of the human heart."[8] McDannell and Lang elaborate on the theocentric model:

> Heavenly existence means a life free not only from the pains of earth but from everything earthly. Not only do sorrow, illness, death, and labor cease, but friends, family, change, and human creativity are utterly unimportant.... Since only the perfect exists in heaven, there is no need for change.... By subscribing to a theocentric model, the question of what the saints do for eternity falls by the wayside. The saints do not have to *do* anything, they merely experience the fullness of their being by existing with God.[9]

It is not surprising that McDannell and Lang regard the theocentric model as "a sparse picture of eternity" and prefer an anthropocentric model.[10]

Extremely spiritualized views of Heaven tend to be just as anthropocentric as the materialized views. The theocentric view of Heaven is tilted toward the spiritualized side but not extremely so.

Heaven Only Knows!

If we are to know anything about Heaven and Hell, we need a truly reliable source. The only such source is the Bible. The reason is simply this: the Bible was inspired by the God of Heaven, and its primary purpose is to reveal to us how we can live forever with that God. John Wesley admirably voiced the importance of the Bible in this regard:

> I want to know one thing, the way to heaven — how to land safe on that happy shore. God himself has condescended to teach the way: for this very end he came down from heaven. He hath written it down in a book. O give me that book! At any price give me the Book of God! I have it. Here is knowledge enough for me. Let me be *homo unius libri* [a man of one book].[11]

Wesley, we should point out, was not an ignorant or uneducated person. He greatly valued education and read voraciously. His confession that he was "a man of one book" (the Bible) did not mean that he ignored other books or even other approaches to knowledge, such as science or philosophy. Wesley recognized, however, that if we want to know about spiritual, transcendent realities beyond our universe, we need revelation. If we want to know about Heaven, we will need to hear from Heaven. And we have heard — in God's revelation to us in the Bible. No better source of information is available.

When we turn to the Bible, we will find a view of Heaven that is neither anthropocentric nor theocentric (as McDannell and Lang use those terms). We will also find a view of Heaven that is neither predominantly spiritualized nor materialized. In this book, we will propose a way of thinking about Heaven that overcomes these opposite tendencies and that is faithful to the teachings of the Bible.

SENSE

The Bible tells us what we need to know about Heaven and Hell.

NONSENSE

Whatever you believe about Heaven is fine.

Chapter 2

THE FIRST PERSON YOU MEET IN HEAVEN

To understand Heaven — and Hell — you must understand Jesus.

Christianity, as the name indicates, is all about Christ. The Lord Jesus Christ is the central figure, the Main Man, of the Christian faith. He is not merely its founder, like Muhammad as the founder of Islam or Moses as the founder of Judaism. Jesus is not only the founder of Christianity, he is its foundation. It's all about him.

If we are to think properly about Heaven, Hell, and other matters relating to them, we must think about them in relation to Christ.[1] In this chapter, we're going to provide an introduction to thinking about these subjects in a Christian — that is, Christ-centered — way. In the rest of this book, we'll be going into more detail, looking more closely at contested biblical passages and their meanings and defending the views outlined here.

Jesus Came from Heaven

Christians associate Jesus Christ with Heaven in a number of ways. Fundamental to our view of Jesus is that though he was really and truly a man, he was not *merely* a man. Rather, Jesus was the Son of God, come down from Heaven. The Nicene Creed affirms that Jesus Christ, "for us human beings and for our salvation, came down from heaven, and became incarnate by the Holy Spirit of the virgin Mary, and was made human."[2] That Jesus came down from Heaven

16

to become a human being tells us several essential things we need to know about Heaven.

(1) *Jesus is the only human being who lived in Heaven before becoming human.* The idea that we all lived in Heaven as spirits and then came down to Earth as human beings is a romantic fiction contradicted by Scripture. For example, John the Baptist affirmed that "the one who comes from above," namely, Jesus, "is above all," whereas "the one who is of the earth belongs to the earth and speaks about earthly things. The one who comes from heaven is above all" (John 3:31). We have discussed this point in some detail in another book.[3]

(2) *Jesus knew more about Heaven than anyone else who has ever lived.* Since Jesus was the only human being who came from Heaven, he could speak authoritatively about what it would take for a person to have a right relationship with the God of Heaven and be assured of living forever in his heavenly kingdom. Jesus didn't need to have a near-death experience to tell us about Heaven; he knew all about it because he had been there. Note these words of Jesus:

> Very truly, I tell you, we speak of what we know and testify to what we have seen; yet you do not receive our testimony. If I told you about earthly things and you do not believe, how can you believe if I tell you about heavenly things? no one has ascended into heaven except the one who descended from heaven, the Son of Man. (John 3:11–13)

(3) *Heaven is not a state of our minds, but a real spiritual realm populated by personal beings.* Above all, Jesus spoke of God as a divine Person in Heaven. He instructed his disciples to pray, "Our Father in heaven" (Matt. 6:9). Jesus himself came down from Heaven, the Son sent by his Father on a mission (John 3:13, 31; 6:38; see also 10:36; 1 John 4:14). The popular mind science and New Age notions of Heaven as a "state of mind" or "higher consciousness" do not take seriously the view of Heaven that Jesus represents.

Jesus Came to Save Us from Hell

The Bible does not teach that Jesus came to tell us to be good boys and girls, to play nice with each other, and to try to get along. Nor did Jesus come with a message of comfort for everyone, an assurance that God loves everybody just the way they are and expects to welcome everyone Home in whatever way they choose to get there.

Rather, as the Gospels make abundantly clear, Jesus had some harsh words to say to a lot of people. He saw his mission in life as essentially an emergency rescue operation. He once said, "For the Son of Man came to seek out and to save the lost" (Luke 19:10). He did this by dying on the cross to pay the price for our sins: "The Son of Man came not to be served, but to serve, and to give his life a ransom for many" (Matt. 20:28; Mark 10:45). Jesus' mission to save us reveals crucial information we need to know about Heaven and Hell.

(1) *People are unfit for Heaven.* Jesus came to save human beings, not from aliens or poverty or pollution or the Roman government, but from themselves — from the evil that is in all of us. We are "lost" because we have gone our own way, like the prodigal son (Luke 15:11–32). Jesus said that people are "evil" (John 3:19); he even told his own disciples that they were "evil" (Matt. 7:11; Luke 11:13)! The human heart, he warned, produces "evil intentions, murder, adultery, fornication, theft, false witness, slander" (Matt. 15:19; Mark 7:22).

> Jesus saw his mission in life as essentially an emergency rescue operation.

But Heaven is the realm of God, who, unlike us, is good (Matt. 19:17; Mark 10:18; Luke 18:19) and perfect (Matt. 5:48). God holds us here on Earth to the standard met in Heaven, that of doing God's will (Matt. 6:10). Although we all fail to meet that standard, God cares about us, and that is why he sent his Son into the world to save us from our corrupt natures.

(2) *Humankind's default destination is Hell, not Heaven.* The belief that everyone or at least nearly everyone will make it into God's eternal kingdom is naïve. It is popular today to wring our hands over the idea of God condemning or rejecting anyone. The biblical view is different; the idea of God forgiving and accepting anyone is what should surprise us. We imagine that in order to

deserve Hell we must go out of our way to be especially obnoxious, and that to deserve Heaven we just need to be reasonably decent people.

That picture is 180 degrees out of phase with the biblical view of the human condition. Human beings are lost and need to be rescued. Change nothing—just continue as you always have, and do whatever comes naturally—and you will remain lost. To escape condemnation and eternal loss, something must change, and God must change it.

If we take Jesus' teaching seriously, we are all Hell-bound unless God does something to intervene. According to Jesus, anyone who calls another person an idiot[4] is deserving of "the hell of fire" (Matt. 5:22).[5] How many of us can claim not to deserve Hell in light of this one saying? Jesus warned that if you are tempted to sin with your hand, foot, or eye, you would be better off to enter God's kingdom without those body parts than to have them and go to Hell (Matt. 5:29–30; 18:9; Mark 9:43–47). Since we have all yielded to such temptations and sinned with our hands, feet, and eyes, we are all Hell-bound unless God does something to stop it.

Jesus even denounced the Pharisees as "hypocrites" and warned that any convert they made was likely to be "twice as much a child of hell" as they were (Matt. 23:15). Many of us are used to thinking of the Pharisees as notoriously bad people, but in fact the Pharisees were widely regarded in their day as the most pious, godly, religiously faithful people in Judaism. The point Jesus is making is not that the Pharisees were especially bad, but that even they were not good enough: "For I tell you, unless your righteousness exceeds that of the scribes and Pharisees, you will never enter the kingdom of heaven" (Matt. 5:20). Jesus' denunciations of the Pharisees has a chilling implication: if *they* can't be good enough, no one can! If anyone is saved, it's a miracle.

(3) *There is a Hell.* Christians may offer a variety of reasons or explanations for Hell, but there is one fundamental reason for Christians to affirm its terrible reality: our Lord, Jesus Christ, says so. Can we explain the moral justification for Hell? Maybe, but our belief that the wicked will go to Hell should not depend on our

ability to explain it. We should begin with the premise that "the Judge of all the earth" will "do what is just" (Gen. 18:25) and then accept whatever judgment he chooses to make. If Jesus had said that everyone would be saved, we would accept it; but he said nothing of the sort. As we have seen, Jesus talked about Hell as a reality that we should avoid at all costs.

(4) *Jesus is the only way to escape Hell.* Let's be clear on this. Jesus did not come in order to narrow the field of people who would be granted eternal life. Jesus came to open up the way—to *be* the Way—to eternal life with God the Father. "I am the way, and the truth, and the life. No one comes to the Father except through me" (John 14:6). The world was already under judgment, and Jesus came to lift that judgment for those who believe in him. "For God so loved the world that he gave his only Son, so that everyone who believes in him may not perish but may have eternal life. Indeed, God did not send the Son into the world to condemn the world, but in order that the world might be saved through him" (John 3:16–17).

The New Testament contemplates no other way of salvation for humanity than Jesus Christ: "And there is salvation in no one else; for there is no other name under heaven that has been given among men by which we must be saved" (Acts 4:12 NASB). When you think about it, if God sent his Son into the world to be rejected, tortured, and killed, all for the purpose of saving us, our situation must be dire indeed. Evidently there was no easier, less painful way for God to reconcile us to himself. If anyone is saved, Jesus saves them.

(5) *Everyone saved before Jesus came was saved by what he did for them.* If Jesus is the only Savior, the only way of salvation, then he must be the source of salvation even for those whom God accepted before Jesus came. Specifically, believers in the Lord God in Old Testament times who could not have known about Jesus were nevertheless saved by Jesus. As David prayed, "For You, O Lord, are good and forgiving, abounding in steadfast love to all who call on you" (Ps. 86:5). By appealing to the Lord and trusting in him to be merciful and forgive them, Old Testament believers were saved. What the New Testament reveals is that Jesus is the Lord who saved them and us:

If you confess with your lips that Jesus is Lord and believe in your heart that God raised him from the dead, you will be saved.... For there is no distinction between Jew and Greek; the same Lord is Lord of all and is generous to all who call on him. For, "Everyone who calls on the name of the Lord shall be saved." (Rom. 10:9, 12–13, quoting Joel 2:32)

Jesus Died and Rose Again

The death and resurrection of Jesus Christ are the central events, the core facts, of the Christian faith. With regard to "the gospel," the apostle Paul states, it is "of first importance ... that Christ died for our sins in accordance with the scriptures, and that he was buried, and that he was raised on the third day in accordance with the scriptures, and that he appeared ..." (1 Cor. 15:3–5). Everything we believe about death, life after death, Heaven, and Hell is related in some way to the death and resurrection of Christ.

(1) *Death is real.* While it seems obvious that death is real, the notion that it is an illusion or simply a natural passage from one stage of life to another is widespread in our culture. Against all theories of death as illusory, the Bible flatly declares that Christ died (1 Cor. 15:3; cf. Rom. 5:6, 8; 1 Thess. 4:14; 1 Pet. 3:18). Death is not only real, it is a terrible "enemy" (1 Cor. 15:26) that must be defeated.

> Everything we believe about death, life after death, Heaven, and Hell is related in some way to the death and resurrection of Christ.

(2) *Christ has defeated death.* The joyous message of the New Testament is that by his own death Christ has defeated death on our behalf:

> Since therefore, the children share flesh and blood, he himself likewise shared the same things, so that through death he might destroy the one who has the power of death, that is, the devil, and free those who all their lives were held in slavery by the fear of death. (Heb. 2:14–15)

Christ has defeated death, not merely by dying, but by dying and then rising from the dead. He who was and is Life incarnate (see John 1:4; 5:26), "the Prince of life" (Acts 3:15 NASB), died but could not be kept dead: "But God raised Him up again, putting an end to the agony of death, since it was impossible for Him to be held in its power" (2:24 NASB). His triumph over death in his resurrection assures us who believe in him that we also will be liberated from death. Even before he died, Jesus told his followers: "I am the resurrection and the life. The one who believes in me will live even if he dies, and the one who lives and believes in me will never die" (John 11:25 – 26 NET).

(3) *Human beings exist in some form after death.* We are not told much in the Bible about the condition or state of the dead. But as we will show in detail later in this book, the Bible does teach that the dead continue to exist in some kind of spiritual state.

One way we know this truth is that Jesus, who was fully human, existed after his physical death. While he was hanging on the cross to die, Jesus promised one of the two criminals who were crucified alongside him that he would be in Paradise with him that very day (Luke 23:43). Between his death and resurrection, when he was "alive in the spirit," Christ "went and made a proclamation to the spirits in prison" (1 Pet. 3:19). Although there is an ongoing debate about who those spirits were and what Christ proclaimed to them, the text does clearly indicate that he existed in spirit form between his death and resurrection.[6]

(4) *The Christian hope is resurrection, not bodiless life after death.* God created us to be human, corporeal beings, and whatever existence we might have beyond the grave as incorporeal spirits is unnatural and unfulfilling to us. The message of Jesus' resurrection is not that there is "life after death" but that life has conquered death. Our salvation will not be complete until God has raised us from the dead to immortal, embodied life as glorified human beings. That is why belief in Christ's own resurrection is so crucial to the Christian faith. "If there is no resurrection of the dead, then Christ has not been raised; and if Christ has not been raised, then

our proclamation has been in vain and your faith has been in vain" (1 Cor. 15:13–14).

(5) *Our resurrection bodies will be like Christ's.* If we want to get some idea what we will be like in our resurrected state, we should take the risen Jesus as our example. The apostle Paul tells us that "the Lord Jesus Christ ... will transform our lowly bodies so that they will be like his glorious body" (Phil. 3:21 NIV). "Just as we have borne the image of the man of dust, we will also bear the image of the man of heaven" (1 Cor. 15:49).

(6) *In the resurrection we will be glorified, immortal people.* The New Testament reveals that Jesus' resurrection state—and, in the future, ours—is both like and unlike what we now experience as "normal" human life. On the one hand, Jesus is still a man, a male human being (Acts 17:31; 1 Cor. 15:47; 1 Tim. 2:5). He can still eat and drink (Luke 24:42–43; Acts 10:41). He can still be touched (Luke 24:39; John 20:17, 27; 1 John 1:1). He still has flesh and bones (Luke 24:39). He has hands, feet, and a side which, when he appeared to his disciples, still bore marks left behind from his crucifixion ordeal (Luke 24:39–40; John 20:20, 25, 27). Our expectation is that in the resurrection we will also retain our identity, our gender, our human form, and our capacities to touch, feel, eat, drink, and interact with other beings.

On the other hand, Jesus is now immortal, incapable of ever dying again (Rom. 6:9–10; 1 Tim. 6:16). When Jesus appeared to his disciples, he often appeared and disappeared suddenly, even in a room behind locked doors (Luke 24:31, 36; John 20:19, 26). He is a "heavenly" person, a "life-giving spirit" (1 Cor. 15:45, 47–49). He is, in fact, living in Heaven, where he will stay until it is time for him to return (Acts 3:19–21).

Likewise, believers are promised that in the resurrection their current state of mortality, corruption, weakness, and humility will be exchanged for a state of immortality, incorruptibility, power, and glory (Luke 20:36; 1 Cor. 15:42–44; Phil. 3:21). We will still be the same persons, but we will be dramatically, radically changed (1 Cor. 15:51–52). In the resurrection our lives will no longer be characterized by the cycle of being born, growing up, getting married, having children, and dying; in these respects, at least, we will be like the angels in Heaven (Luke 20:34–36). Instead of merely natural, biological life, we will possess supernatural life empowered by the Spirit, fully bearing the image of the heavenly Man (1 Cor. 15:44–49).

We don't understand everything about our future life after the resurrection. It is a form of life we have never seen, except historically in the glimpses of Jesus' risen life. We can be assured, though, that we will be glorified with him, and as a result, we will be like him in every way that a human being can and should be like him — strong, immortal, holy, and perfect in every human virtue. We will be conformed to the image of Jesus Christ, God's Son (Rom. 8:17, 29; 1 John 3:1–2). But before this hope is finally realized, Jesus must do something else for us.

Jesus Is Coming Again

The Christian expectation for the future should focus especially on one crucial event: "the blessed hope and glorious appearing of our great God and Savior Jesus Christ" (Titus 2:13 NKJV). The traditional Jewish belief in the ancient world (and still to this day in Judaism) was that the Messiah would come once to bring judgment on the enemies of God and of Israel and to inaugurate the age to come. The death, resurrection, and exaltation of Jesus the Messiah to Heaven required his first-century Jewish followers to adjust their theology in these matters.[7] The Messiah has come and gone, but is coming again.

> But now he has appeared once for all at the end of the ages to do away with sin by the sacrifice of himself. Just as man is destined to die once, and after that to face judgment, so Christ was sacrificed once to take away the sins of many people; and he will appear a second time, not to bear sin, but to bring salvation to those who are waiting for him. (Heb. 9:26–28 NIV)

The future coming of Christ is rich with significance for our understanding of Heaven and Hell.

(1) *Jesus will preside over the Final Judgment.* It is Jesus Christ who will judge all people at the end of history (Matt. 25:31–46;

John 5:21–29; Acts 10:42; 17:31; 2 Cor. 5:10; 2 Tim. 4:1). Before you can even enter into Heaven, you will have to stand before Jesus and submit to his eternal decision. Although we don't pretend to know precisely how things will unfold after death, in a real sense Jesus will be the first Person you will meet in Heaven—and the last, unless he accepts you as one of his people.

Remember, this is the same person who said that anyone insulting his neighbor or giving into temptation with his eye or hand will deserve to be cast into a fiery Hell. This is the same person who warned that very religious people who did many noble, impressive works in his name might hear him say to them, "I never knew you. Away from me, you evildoers!" (Matt. 7:23 NIV). If you are counting on Jesus to be a pushover, an old softie, think again. Jesus will be as stern in his condemnation as he will be generous in his mercy. It is absolutely crucial to make sure now that we are on the Lord's side.

The proof that he is coming again in judgment is that he rose from the dead, victorious over death and all the forces of evil. Jesus told the apostle John, "Do not be afraid; I am the first and the last, and the living one. I was dead, and see, I am alive forever and ever; and I have the keys of Death and of Hades" (Rev. 1:17–18). Jesus holds the keys to our future.

(2) *Jesus will remain human even in executing the Final Judgment.* The apostle Paul told the people of Athens, "God ... has fixed a day in which He will judge the world in righteousness through a Man whom He has appointed, having furnished proof to all men by raising Him from the dead" (Acts 17:30–31 NASB). That man, as we have seen, is Jesus. Although Jesus is the Son of God, by having become a man and remaining human he is, in a real sense, one of us. Certainly, God would be able to judge all people justly even if he had never become incarnate, but his having done so gives his role in judgment an added layer of credibility.

(3) *The eternal home for God's people will be a glorified new heaven and new earth.* If God's intention was for the redeemed to live forever as disembodied spirits in Heaven forever, it would seem unnecessary for Jesus to come back to Earth. When saved people

died, they would simply go to Heaven, and those not saved would not get there. When everyone got where they were supposed to go, the Earth and perhaps the universe in its entirety would be annihilated and Heaven would be all that remained. But such a view of the eternal state of the redeemed is not in keeping with the doctrines of the bodily resurrection and second coming of Jesus Christ.

According to the Bible, the eternal home of God's people will be in a "new heavens and a new earth" (Isa. 65:17; 66:22; 2 Pet. 3:13; Rev. 21:1). The chief differences between this new heavens and new earth and the universe we have now is that the new one will be characterized by righteousness (2 Pet. 3:13) and will not have sin, death, or mourning (Rev. 21:1, 4). This new universe will not happen by redeemed humanity going to live where God is, but by God coming to live where we are: "Behold, the tabernacle of God is among men, and He will dwell among them, and they shall be His people, and God Himself will be among them" (Rev. 21:3 NASB).

What we often call simply "Heaven," then, in reference to the eternal home of God's people, might be better called the New Heavens and New Earth. It will be a place where glorified people will live in immortal bodies with both heavenly and earthly aspects. It will be a place suitable for Jesus Christ, the Heavenly Man, and all those made like him.

SENSE
Heaven means living forever with Jesus, the risen, Heavenly Man.

NONSENSE
We can understand Heaven and Hell without Jesus.

Chapter 3

SPEAKING OF HEAVENS AND HELLS

"Heaven" has three meanings and "hell" has two. Don't get them confused!

Anyone who has studied a second language—or even studied his or her first language carefully—notices that languages have a penchant for using the same word in a variety of different meanings. You could probably come up with a list of five or more meanings for the English word *trunk* without consulting a dictionary. The word *bar* has a dizzying variety of uses: you can have high jump bars, jailhouse bars, candy bars, sand bars, or soap bars; bars can be stripes on a uniform, lines separating measures in sheet music, a place that sells drinks, an association of lawyers, a measure of atmospheric pressure, or a mark indicating a repeating decimal.

This fact about human language applies to words we use in matters of religious or spiritual significance. *Sanctify* sometimes means an act of consecration or dedication to God, and sometimes means a process of becoming more conformed to God's moral character. The word *ark* refers either to Noah's boat or to the chest carried by Israelite priests in its early history (the "ark of the covenant"). Paul can use the phrase *the righteousness of God* to refer to God's own just character that assures us that his judgments are above reproach (Rom. 3:5) and the next time use it to refer to God's gracious gift of being accounted just before him through faith in Jesus Christ (3:21–22; see also 1:17). Human language exhibits such flexibility even in the Bible, a fact that otherwise reasonable people all too easily ignore by trying tooshoehorn one meaning or usage into every occurrence of a word.

Our topic of Heaven and Hell is considerably complicated, and people often get confused by the fact that both of these words do double or even triple duty in the Bible. We will therefore give some attention here to how these words are used in Scripture.

Heaven of Heavens

The Hebrew word commonly translated "heaven" is *shāmayim*. Oddly enough, *shāmayim* is a plural form and only occurs in that form in the Old Testament except in the expression "the heaven of heavens" (Deut. 10:14; 1 Kings 8:27; 2 Chron. 2:5; 6:18; yet see Ps. 115:16, "the heavens of heavens"). Hebrew often used plural nouns where no literal plural was meant and where in English we would expect a singular noun. That is why in some English translations you will see "heaven" and in others "heavens" rendering the same word in the same verse (e.g., Gen. 1:1). The Greek word for heaven, *ouranos*, occurs in both singular and plural forms. The Greek translation of the Old Testament sometimes uses the singular form to translate the Hebrew plural (again, see Gen. 1:1). But the New Testament sometimes uses a plural form, even when it is not quoting the Old Testament, in imitation of the Old Testament idiom.

Why is this important to know? Because we should not read into the simple plural form "heavens" the notion that there are several separate "heavens" or spiritual realms. For example, when Matthew reports that Jesus spoke of "the kingdom of the heavens" (Matt. 5:3, translating the Greek literally), he is simply reflecting the common Hebrew idiom, not alluding to a group of distinct "heavens" in God's kingdom. This is why almost all English Bibles translate this expression as "the kingdom of heaven."

The Hebrew and Greek words for heaven have at least three clearly distinguishable uses in the Bible. (1) *Shāmayim* and *ouranos* can refer to the *sky*, the heaven of the air—the environment of air, clouds, and rain, where birds fly (e.g., Gen. 1:20, 26, 28; 8:2; Deut. 28:12; Ps. 147:8; Matt. 8:20; 13:32; 16:2–3).

(2) These words can refer to *space*, the heaven of space—the physical "heavens" beyond our own world, where the sun, moon, and stars exist (e.g., Gen. 1:14, 15, 17; 15:5; Deut. 4:19; 28:62; Acts 2:19–20; Heb. 11:12). Although these two uses are distinguishable, the distinction is not a sharp or rigid one in the Bible. The "heavens" in either of these senses are physical realms visible (in part) from our vantage point on the Earth.

(3) Both words can refer to the *spiritual realm*, the heaven of spirit, where God and the angels associate (e.g., Deut. 26:15; 1 Kings 8:30; Ps. 14:2; Matt. 6:9–10; 18:10; 28:2). It used to be a given in Christian theology that this Heaven was sharply distinguished from the heavens of air and space, but we can no longer assume this point to be either understood or accepted.

A key text that provides some orientation to the subject is Paul's statement that in Christ "all things in heaven and on earth were created, things visible and invisible" (Col. 1:16).[1] Paul here divides created reality into two parts: "heaven," which is the realm of the "invisible" things, and the "earth," which is the realm of the "visible" things. Since the birds in the sky and the sun, moon, and stars (or at least many of them) are visible to human eyes, the realm of "the invisible" here is implicitly understood to transcend the physical heavens. Its regular occupants are beings of "spirit," that is, intrinsically incorporeal beings—God (John 4:20–24) and the angels (Heb. 1:7).[2]

We do not deny that corporeal beings can in some way become present in Heaven, just as we do not deny that some incorporeal beings are present (and can even become visible) in our physical world. (We will have more to say about corporeal beings in Heaven

MORTIMER J. ADLER

Heaven being the dwelling place of God, preeminently a purely spiritual being, it cannot be regarded as a physical place, a space that can be occupied by bodies. It is not out there or up there or anywhere that has a location in the physical cosmos.[3]

later in this book.) However, incorporeal, spiritual beings are "native" to Heaven, just as corporeal, physical beings are "native" to Earth and the rest of the physical universe.

Physical Heavens	Spiritual Heaven
Designed for physical occupants (spiritual beings can visit)	Designed for spiritual occupants (physical beings can visit)
birds / sun, moon, stars	God / angels
normally visible	normally invisible

Hades, Hell, and Sheol

Far greater confusion has swirled around the meaning of the term *hell*, in large part because of a peculiar feature of the King James Version (KJV), which translates *two different Greek words* in the New Testament as "hell."

The first of these Greek words is *Hadēs*. The Greeks used Hades to refer to the realm of the dead, a place of "eternal retirement" where the spirits of the dead exist forever as less substantial—and generally less happy—versions of their human selves. Persons existed in Hades, but it was not an existence to which one looked forward. Homer's famous line is to the point: "I would rather be a paid servant in a poor man's house and be above ground than king of kings among the dead."[4]

Seventh-day Adventists and Jehovah's Witnesses, both of whom deny that the soul continues to exist in an afterlife, agree that Hades in Greek usage referred to an underworld or netherworld. The Adventist scholar Samuele Bacchiocchi, for example, states that "*hades* in Greek mythology is the underworld," and he recognizes that this idea was current in the Judaism of Jesus' day:

> The souls of the righteous proceeded immediately after death to heavenly felicity, there to await the resurrection, while the souls of the godless went to a place of torment in *hades*. The popular acceptance of this scenario is reflected in the Parable of the Rich Man and Lazarus.[5]

In the parable[6] of the rich man and Lazarus, the rich man dies and goes to Hades, where he suffers torment in flames, while the poor man Lazarus is carried by angels to "Abraham's bosom," a place of rest for the righteous. The rich man asks Abraham to let Lazarus dip his finger in some water to cool his tongue; when he is told that is impossible, he asks Abraham to send Lazarus to warn his brothers about the place of torment. Abraham answers, "If they do not listen to Moses and the prophets, neither will they be convinced even if someone rises from the dead" (Luke 16:19–31).

Bacchiocchi gives several reasons why the parable cannot be taken literally (disembodied souls do not have bodies that can feel pain or dip fingers in water; a literal conversation between Abraham and the rich man across the divide seems impossible; etc.) and concludes that Jesus was using the popular notions about Hades and Abraham's bosom as a setting for his story without endorsing any of those concepts.[7] That may be; but it doesn't change the fact that the term *Hades* in this passage clearly means a netherworld or underworld where the dead exist.

Since this was its regular meaning in ancient Greek, it should be assumed to have that meaning elsewhere in the New Testament unless the texts specifically disavow such a meaning. Opponents of the traditional Christian view, then, bear the burden of proof with regard to the meaning of Hades. It is not sufficient for them to show that a particular occurrence doesn't make explicit that the dead continue to exist in Hades; they must show that the word doesn't have that meaning in the New Testament.

Outside this controversial use in the parable of Lazarus and the rich man, the word Hades is used in a small number of other New Testament texts. In one saying Jesus warns the city of Capernaum that far from being "exalted to heaven," it "will be brought down to Hades" (Matt. 11:23; Luke 10:15). This saying is certainly consistent with the conventional Greek use of the term Hades to refer to the underworld. In another saying, Jesus promises that "the gates of Hades" will not prevail against his church (Matt. 16:18). The metaphor pictures the underworld, the realm of the dead, as a place with gates to keep the dead from escaping. Bacchiocchi in effect admits this, without noting its implications.[8]

In the book of Revelation, "Death and Hades" are consistently linked together (Rev. 1:18; 6:8; 20:13–14) without any clear explanation. What is clear is that Hades is distinct from the final, eternal punishment of the wicked, because at the end death and Hades are "thrown into the lake of fire" (Rev. 20:13–14). But this does not preclude Hades being an "intermediate" realm in which the wicked suffer while awaiting their final disposition.

In the first Christian sermon, the apostle Peter uses the word Hades twice in reference to the death of Jesus:

> But God raised him up, having freed him from death, because it was impossible for him to be held in its power. For David says concerning him,
>
>> "I saw the Lord always before me,
>>   for he is at my right hand so that I will not be shaken;
>> therefore my heart was glad, and my tongue rejoiced;
>>   moreover my flesh will live in hope.
>> *For you will not abandon my soul to Hades,*
>>   *or let your Holy One experience corruption.*
>> You have made known to me the ways of life;
>>   you will make me full of gladness with your presence."
>
> Fellow Israelites, I may say to you confidently of our ancestor David that he both died and was buried, and his tomb is with us to this day. Since he was a prophet, he knew that God had sworn with an oath to him that he would put one of his descendants on his throne. Foreseeing this, David spoke of the resurrection of the Messiah, saying,
>
>> *"He was not abandoned to Hades,*
>>   *nor did his flesh experience corruption."*
>
> This Jesus God raised up, and of that all of us are witnesses. (Acts 2:24–32)

This is the one passage in the New Testament that uses Hades in a quotation from the Old Testament. The Hebrew word for which Hades is substituted is *Sheol*. According to Bacchiocchi (and other advocates of the same view), "*hades* was used in the Greek world in a vastly different way than *sheol*,"[9] which was a term for the grave. But since Hades is here (and in the Greek translations of the Old Testament used by ancient Jews) used to translate Sheol, the conclusion is drawn that we should understand Hades to mean essentially what Sheol meant—which, we are told, was simply the grave.

This line of argument, though extremely common and apparently persuasive to many, is seriously flawed. If indeed Hades in Greek thought meant something "vastly different" from Sheol, and if Sheol simply meant the grave, why would the Greek Old Testament translators (and Luke) use Hades in place of Sheol (since other Greek words were available)? Assuming the Old Testament translators made a mistake, would Luke perpetuate that mistake in his inspired writing? Could we not argue the reverse—that if these translators and Luke thought Hades was a serviceable translation of Sheol, then the words were at least roughly synonymous?

Many Old Testament scholars now think that Sheol was typically not another designation for the grave but was in fact more frequently a term for the underworld. Not everyone agrees; in fact, the NIV, following the view of one of its translators, R. Laird Harris, usually translates Sheol as "grave."[10] However, the evidence suggests that such a translation should be the exception rather than the rule.

One of the most graphic and significant pictures of Sheol in the Old Testament comes from the wilderness experiences of Israel. Unbelieving Israelites in Korah's rebellion were punished when the ground opened up and they went "down alive into Sheol" (Num. 16:30, 33). Later, Moses warns the Israelites that God's anger kindles a fire that "burns to the depths of Sheol" (Deut. 32:22). Even the NIV here reads, "burns to the realm of death below." Sheol is sometimes mentioned in parallel with "the Pit" (Ps. 30:3; Prov. 1:12; Isa. 14:15; 38:18; Ezek. 31:16), recalling the judgment on Korah's rebellion.

It is striking how often the Old Testament speaks of Sheol as if it were the distinctively appropriate end of the wicked, an expression of God's wrath and judgment.[11] "The wicked shall depart to

Sheol, all the nations that forget God" (Ps. 9:17; see also 31:17; 55:15; 89:46–48; Prov. 5:5; 7:27; 9:18; 14:12; 16:25). By contrast, the righteous going to Sheol, when it is contemplated, is usually characterized as wrong, and hope is often held out for deliverance from Sheol (Ps. 16:10; 18:5; 30:3; 86:13; Prov. 15:24; Hos. 13:14). These two ideas are sometimes brought together:

> As sheep they are appointed for Sheol;
> Death shall be their shepherd;
> And the upright shall rule over them in the morning,
> And their form shall be for Sheol to consume
> So that they have no habitation.
> But God will redeem my soul from the power of Sheol,
> For He will receive me. (Ps. 49:14–15 NASB)

In Isaiah, the dead are clearly pictured as spirits or "shades" existing in Sheol:

> Sheol beneath is stirred up
>   to meet you when you come;
> it rouses the shades [*rephaîm*] to greet you,
>   all who were leaders of the earth;
> it raises from their thrones
>   all who were kings of the nations.
> All of them will speak
>   and say to you:
> "You too have become as weak as we!
>   You have become like us!"
> Your pomp is brought down to Sheol,
>   and the sound of your harps;
> maggots are the bed beneath you,
>   and worms are your covering. (Isa. 14:9–11)

Now let's go back to Peter's use of the term Hades in his first Christian sermon. He is quoting Psalm 16:10, where David affirms confidently that God will not abandon his soul to Sheol or allow him to undergo decay. Adventists and Jehovah's Witnesses urge that the parallel between Sheol and decay proves that Sheol is the grave. But this simply does not follow. David is expressing the hope, actually realized by Jesus the Son of David on behalf of all who believe, of escape from death. He expresses this hope by saying two closely related but not identical things: that God will not abandon his soul to Sheol, and that God will not allow him to undergo decay.

When Peter applies this passage to Jesus, it is not even entirely clear that he means that Jesus actually went to Hades. What he says is that God did not abandon or forsake Jesus "to Hades." This *could* mean that Jesus went to Hades but didn't stay there. Some Christians think so, and they conclude either that Hades had a blessed place for the righteous, where Christ would have gone, or that Christ went to Hades to announce to the unrighteous his triumph over sin and death. Or it could mean that God didn't abandon Christ by consigning him to Hades. If this view is correct, then Christ did not go to Hades at all. Either way, the passage is consistent with the view that Hades is the underworld, where the spirits of the dead continue to exist in some way.

We conclude, then, that the terms Sheol and Hades refer to the underworld, the abode of the dead as they await their final disposition at the Last Judgment.

Gehenna and Hell

The other Greek word translated "hell" in the KJV (and in some other Bibles as well) is *Gehenna*. The term Gehenna comes from the Hebrew place name *gê-hinnōm*, "valley of Hinnom," also known as the "valley of the son of Hinnom," which was first mentioned in Joshua 15:8; 18:16. During the years prior to the Babylonian exile, this valley (located just south of Jerusalem) became "infamous for the pagan rites, especially child sacrifice, that

> Gehenna is to be distinguished from Hades, which is an unpleasant intermediate abode for the dead, particularly the unrighteous dead, as they await consignment to Gehenna.

were offered there" (cf. 2 Kings 16:3; 23:10; Jer. 19:6–7).[12] In Judaism in the two centuries before Jesus, Gehenna came to be used as a picture of the final judgment on the wicked. In other words, Jesus didn't invent this term or its use to refer to Hell; he took it over from the Judaism of his day.

It is commonly said that in Jesus' day, Gehenna was the place where refuse from the city of Jerusalem was dumped and burned— the city dump. Some writers who deny eternal torment for the wicked in Hell claim that the metaphor of the city dump favors the view that the wicked are simply destroyed in Hell. However, various scholars have pointed out that the basis for this view of Hell as the city dump comes from a medieval source dating to about AD 1200—far too late to take seriously.[13]

Jesus used Gehenna to picture the final judgment of the wicked, a place where they would gnash their teeth, where the fire would never go out, and where the worms would never die. As we will argue later, this is a picture of unending punishment for the wicked. In any case, Gehenna is to be distinguished from Hades, which is an unpleasant intermediate abode for the dead, particularly the unrighteous dead, as they await consignment to Gehenna. Thus, it is all right to translate Gehenna as "Hell," but it is a mistake to translate Hades as "Hell." Keeping these two terms straight will help us understand better what the Bible says on this "hot" subject.

SENSE

Hades is not Hell.

NONSENSE

Hell is just the grave.

Chapter 4

TILL DEATH DO US PART

When we die, does something survive?

The dispute over the meanings of the words *Sheol* and *Hades* is part of a broader dispute over the question of whether the human spirit or soul continues to exist as a personal entity after physical death. We have already seen that a good case can be made for an affirmative answer to that question. However, the traditional Christian understanding of the Bible on this subject has been subjected to criticism from both scholarly and popular sources on a number of fronts. The good news is that considering this criticism and responding to it will help sharpen our understanding of what the Bible teaches about Heaven and Hell.

The usual term for the belief in continuing human existence after death is the "immortality of the soul." We consider this term rather misleading. However, the idea to which it usually refers in orthodox Christian theology is biblical, as we will demonstrate.

What Is Death?

Although the Bible has a lot to say about life and death, it does not engage in systematic analysis of the topic. The Bible offers no formal definition of "death" and no detailed exposition of what happens to people when they die. We must infer our understanding of death from a whole range of biblical statements pertaining to the subject. In doing so, we must be careful to distinguish idiomatic or euphemistic expressions for death, which may not be intended to communicate anything more than that a person has died, from comments intending to express some specific understanding of what that death involved.

Some of the biblical idioms associated with death include the following: to "expire," or, as we would put it, to breathe one's last (e.g., Luke 23:46); to "depart" (Phil. 1:23); to "be no more" (Ps. 37:10); to be "gathered" to one's people or fathers (Gen. 25:8); to "sleep" (1 Thess. 4:13–15), to "lie down" with one's fathers (Gen. 47:30); to be "cut off," or to be "cut off" from the land, or one's family, or the like (Ps. 37:9); and to "perish" (John 3:16). Although a couple of these idioms might seem to support the idea that death ends all existence for a person ("be no more," possibly "expire"), most of the other idioms imply that a person continues to exist after death ("depart," "sleep," to be "gathered" to one's people, to "lie down" with one's fathers). Notably, the idiom to be "gathered" to one's fathers or people probably reflects the idea of the dead being united with their ancestors in the afterlife.[1] Still, we should be cautious about reading more into these idioms than can be supported from more explicit statements elsewhere.

Religious groups that deny any afterlife, such as the Jehovah's Witnesses, routinely assume without argument that to die means to cease existing. Biblically, though, death means to cease *living*, not to cease *existing*. There is a difference. The most common biblical idiom for death, "cutting off," nicely expresses the basic idea of death as *separation*. To die is to be cut off or separated from those who are living. This is why the Bible can speak of death as physical or spiritual. Physical death cuts a person off from community or interaction with other physical beings in the physical world. Spiritual death cuts a person off from community with God, the Spirit who created us. What the book of Revelation calls "the second death" (Rev. 2:11; 20:6, 14; 21:8) is a final separation of the wicked from the gracious presence of God (cf. 2 Thess. 1:9).

"His Thoughts Perish"

Those who believe that death ends all personal existence do have a battery of biblical texts that they think proves their doctrine. You can rely on these proof texts being taken out of context. Consider, for example, the following commonly cited verse:

> His spirit departs, he returns to the earth;
> In that very day his thoughts perish. (Ps. 146:4 NASB)

Bacchiocchi draws the customary conclusion from Psalm 146:4. "Since at death the 'thoughts perish,' it is evident there is no conscious soul that survives the death of the body."[2] However, Psalm 146:4 does not say that the dead do not exist or even that they do not think, but that when people die their "thoughts perish."

To understand what this means, we should first back up and get a little context. The verse immediately preceding states:

> Do not trust in princes,
> Or in human beings, who cannot deliver! (Ps. 146:3 NET)

The psalmist is saying that we should not trust in princes, or in any other mere human being, because when he dies, "his thoughts perish." In other words, whatever "thoughts" a prince or other human being has that may seem to be potentially helpful to us, they will perish with that person when he dies; this is one reason we should not put our trust in such people. Instead, we should look to God alone for help, because he is the Creator, the One who can and does help the oppressed, hungry, imprisoned, blind, strangers, orphans, and widows, and—unlike the mortal princes who will die—he will reign forever (Ps. 146:5–10).

In this context, the mortal prince's "thoughts" are his plans, his intentions, what he thinks he will do. This usage is common in the Old Testament, especially in the poetic writings (see Ps. 33:10, 11; 56:5; 94:11; Prov. 6:18; 12:5; 15:22, 26; 16:3; 19:21; 20:18). Many translations actually use the word "plans" in some of these verses rather than the more literal "thoughts" (e.g., NET, NIV, NRSV). In English we have an idiom that may even derive from this passage as we sometimes say, "Perish the thought," which means, "I hope that doesn't happen." It has nothing to do with a person ceasing to have any thoughts at all.

So, what the psalmist is saying is that we shouldn't trust in princes or other mortal persons because when they die, their great promises and plans bite the dust along with them. To read into this verse the idea that death is nonexistence is going way beyond what the text actually says.

"The Dead Do Not Know Anything"

Among the biblical proof texts cited to support the doctrine that the soul ceases to exist when the body dies, the most common are probably a couple of passages in Ecclesiastes:

> I said in my heart with regard to human beings that God is testing them to show that they are but animals. For the fate of humans and the fate of animals is the same; as one dies, so dies the other. They all have the same breath, and humans have no advantage over the animals; for all is vanity. All go to one place; all are from the dust, and all turn to dust again. Who knows whether the human spirit goes upward and the spirit of animals goes downward to the earth? (Eccl. 3:18–21)

> It is the same for all, since the same event happens to the righteous and the wicked, to the good and the evil, to the clean and the unclean, to him who sacrifices and him who does not sacrifice. As is the good, so is the sinner, and he who swears is as is he who shuns an oath. This is an evil in all that is done under the sun, that the same event happens to all. Also, the hearts of the children of man are full of evil, and madness is in their hearts while they live, and after that they go to the dead. But he who is joined with all the living has hope, for a living dog is better than a dead lion. For the living know that they will die, but the dead know nothing, and they have no more reward, for the memory of them is forgotten. Their love and their hate and their envy have already perished, and forever they have no more share in all that is done under the sun.…

> Whatever your hand finds to do, do it with all your might; for there is no work or thought or knowledge or wisdom in Sheol, to which you are going. (Eccl. 9:2–6, 10 ESV)

These statements about human beings dying just like animals and the dead not knowing or doing anything are often cited to prove that death means the end of a person's existence. This way of reading these passages, though it seems correct on the surface, fails to come to terms with their meaning in the overall context of the book. The purpose of Ecclesiastes is to reveal the bankruptcy of human wisdom and the need for God's revelation. In the course of making its argument for this truth, this book presents opinions that from an earth-bound, human point of view seem right but that in light of divine revelation are known to be wrong. The book in its entirety is inspired and true; but, like any book of the Bible that quotes fallen human beings (or even the Devil!), not every opinion expressed in the book is true. In a surprising admission of this point, the Jehovah's Witnesses' Bible encyclopedia makes the following comment:

> While some claim that the book contradicts itself, this is only because they do not see that the book many times sets forth the common view as opposed to the view that reflects divine wisdom. (Compare Ec 1:18; 7:11, 12.) So one must read with a view to getting the sense and must keep in mind the theme of the book.[3]

Consider the following list of assertions contained within Ecclesiastes. From a biblical standpoint, all of these statements are *false*. Ecclesiastes reports these statements, not to endorse them but to show what life looks like "under the sun." This key phrase, which occurs thirty-one times in the book (1:3, 9, 14; 2:3, 11, 17–20, 22; 3:16; 4:1, 3, 7, 15; 5:12, 17; 6:1, 5, 12; 8:9, 15ab, 17; 9:3, 6, 9ab, 11, 13; 10:5), expresses the consistent perspective of Solomon, a kind of "worm's-eye view" of things as opposed to a "bird's-eye view" such as only God can give. It marks the earth-bound, limited perspective that frames so many of the book's statements:

- Everything is vanity, that is, a waste of time and effort (1:2, 14; 12:8).
- Nothing new ever happens (1:9–10).
- Wisdom and knowledge are vain because they bring grief and pain (1:17–18).
- The wise person is no better off than the fool (2:14–16; 6:8).

- The best thing to do is eat, drink, and try to be happy (2:24; 8:15; 9:7–9).
- People are mere animals (3:18).
- Better to be dead than alive, and better still to have never existed (4:2–3; 7:1).
- A person dies no better off for all his hard work (2:11; 3:9; 5:16).
- Too much righteousness or wisdom will lead to ruin (7:16).
- The righteous and the wicked will suffer the same fate (9:2).

It is possible to offer some "sanctified" or pious interpretations of some of these statements so that they no longer seem so obviously wrong. But to do so is to miss the point. Solomon means exactly what he says: if you look at life honestly from a mortal human point of view, it all seems so empty. The wise are no better off than the fools, the rich are no better off than the poor, and the righteous are no better off than the wicked (in fact, it pays not to be too righteous or too wicked).

The ultimate proof of this pessimistic outlook is that everybody dies the same death. In fact, human death seems to work the same way as animal death; in the end, we do not appear to be better off than animals. No wonder Solomon begins and climaxes the book with the complaint, "All is vanity" (Eccl. 1:2; 12:8). No wonder he suggests several times that the best we can do is eat, drink, and be merry. Solomon seems to agree with the old beer commercial that said that you only go around once in life, so you should grab for all the gusto you can.

But it isn't true. Human beings are more than animals (Gen. 1:26–27; 2:7). The righteous and wise person is better off than the wicked and foolish person (as almost every verse of the entire book of Proverbs reminds us). There is more to life than eating, drinking, and enjoying our short mortal lives (Rom. 14:17). The only person who would be better off never having existed is the wicked person (cf. Matt. 26:24). The righteous have a bright, joyous future awaiting them (Rom. 8:18–25); the wicked have a dark, fearful future awaiting them (e.g., Heb. 10:26–31). Our hard work is not in vain in the Lord (1 Cor. 15:58).

Now, it is absolutely correct that, in biblical thought, humanity's hope of escape from the bleak picture shown in Ecclesiastes is not what is commonly called "the afterlife." The "good news" of the Bible is not that death is merely a natural passage into a brighter and happier world. That is a false teaching that is prevalent in our society today. Death throughout the Bible is an "enemy" (e.g., 1 Cor. 15:26). The message of the Bible is a mixed message of both good news and bad news. The good news is that through faith in God's merciful provision for our salvation in Jesus Christ we may have hope of resurrection from the dead to eternal and immortal life (1 Cor. 15:12–58; 2 Tim. 1:8–10). The bad news is that those who do not entrust themselves to God's mercy in Christ are already facing a resurrection from the dead to face a judgment worse than physical death (Rev. 20:12–15).

Although the Bible does not place humanity's hope in a universal afterlife, it does not follow that the dead simply cease to exist. Again, this may seem to be what Ecclesiastes says, but on closer inspection it turns out that it does not. Let's look at the two key texts more closely.

(1) "I said in my heart with regard to human beings that God is testing them to show that they are but animals. For the fate of humans and the fate of animals is the same" (Eccl. 3:18–19a). What this says is that from a human point of view there is nothing to which we can look forward after death. Note how Solomon makes his point from an earthly, human point of view rather than from God's point of view (or even that of the departed). The expression "I said to myself" (1:16; 2:1, 15; 3:17, 18) makes it clear that what follows is Solomon's own rumination, not divine revelation. What he says to himself may be true enough, or true from a certain perspective, but it is not the whole truth.

(2) "This is an evil in all that is done under the sun, that the same event happens to all.... For the living know that they will die, but the dead know nothing, and they have no more reward, for the memory of them is forgotten. Their love and their hate and their envy have already perished, and forever they have no more share in all that is done under the sun" (Eccl. 9:3a, 5–6 ESV). Notice that Solomon says

that the dead have no reward. Clearly, from God's point of view this is false; the dead will have a reward, whether blessing or judgment. But Solomon is speaking about how things appear to those who are left behind. Thus, he says that the dead have no more reward because "their memory is forgotten," that is, because the people who remain alive eventually forget about them and move on with their lives.

It is a mistake, then, to take such clauses as "for the dead do not know anything" out of context and conclude that the dead literally have no consciousness or awareness of anything at all, not even of themselves. This is not what Ecclesiastes is teaching. One might just as well claim that the book is teaching that it makes no difference whether a person is righteous and wise or wicked and foolish.

It is interesting to note that Solomon even seems to acknowledge the widespread belief in an afterlife, but can neither confirm nor deny it: "Who knows whether the human spirit goes upward and the spirit of animals goes downward to the earth?" (Eccl. 3:21). The answer is, apart from revelation, no one really can know. This is arguably the point of the book: the wisest man, apart from God's revelation, really has no answers to the big questions in life. Such wisdom merely leads to pessimism and fatalism.

The book of Ecclesiastes, then, makes an invaluable contribution to the canon of Scripture. In it God reveals the bankruptcy of human wisdom apart from God's revelation. Its "death ends it all" theme needs to be interpreted in that context.

If death is not the end of a person's existence, what survives? What continues to exist after a person dies? We will explore that question in the next chapter.

SENSE

Death is the end of a person's life.

NONSENSE

Death is the end of a person's existence.

Chapter 5

SOUL MAN

Is the soul "immortal"?

In 1955 the German theologian Oscar Cullmann gave the Ingersoll Lecture on the Immortality of Man (later called the Ingersoll Lectures on Human Immortality) at Andover Chapel at Harvard University. This century-long lecture series (1896–1995) was one of the most influential of its kind, with such notable speakers in its history as William James, Alfred North Whitehead, Paul Tillich, Elisabeth Kübler-Ross, and Martin E. Marty. Cullmann's lecture was soon published in a Swiss periodical and later published as a short book with the title *Immortality of the Soul or Resurrection of the Dead?* In the preface to this book, Cullmann begins by acknowledging, "No other publication of mine has provoked such enthusiasm or such violent hostility."[1] Ironically, Cullmann's study, though it is subject to some critique, is a valuable and essentially sound presentation of the biblical view of what lies beyond death.

Immortality of the Soul versus the Resurrection of the Dead

Cullmann's thesis is that the doctrine of the immortality of the soul is a pagan Greek belief that, to a great extent, supplanted the biblical doctrine of the resurrection from the dead in popular Christian thought during the nineteenth and twentieth centuries. To those who are used to associating the expression "immortality of the soul" with Christianity, an attack on this doctrine might seem to be an attack on the Christian faith. However, a close examination of Cullmann's argument shows otherwise.

The heart of Cullmann's concern was to refute the notion, becoming increasingly common in Christianity, that belief in the resurrection of the body is not essential to New Testament Christianity but is "simply an accommodation to the mythological expressions of the thought of their time, and that the heart of the matter is the immortality of the soul." In other words, Cullmann's primary target was not traditional, conservative Christianity but liberal Protestant theology, which rejected the historical fact of the resurrection of Jesus and along with it the belief that God will raise human beings from the dead at the end of history.

Predictably, those who believe that the human person ceases to exist altogether at death have cited Cullmann's book in support, often using its title as a kind of slogan while failing to read his argument carefully. The Adventist scholar Samuele Bacchiocchi originally intended to use Cullmann's full title as the title of his own book *Immortality or Resurrection?*[2] The publications of the Jehovah's Witnesses have frequently appealed to Cullmann's work in support of their belief that death means the extinction of the person.[3]

The fact is that Cullmann does not deny the existence of the human person after death and before resurrection. What he denies is a hybrid position that is part Christian, part pagan, according to which death is not an enemy but a friend, the natural release of the soul from its imprisonment in the body and its immediate transport to a perfect afterlife. Cullmann describes the state of the departed believer between his death and future resurrection as "the state of anticipation in which, according to St Paul, the dead in Christ find themselves during their 'sleeping' as they wait for the resurrection of the body." Obviously, someone must *exist* in order to be in a "state of anticipation"! Cullmann simply emphasizes "the provisional and still imperfect character of this state" because the New Testament envisions human life as redeemed only in the resurrection of the body.

In making this argument, Cullmann is not opposing the historic, orthodox doctrine of Christianity but contributing to its defense and revival. The Apostles' Creed climaxes with an affirmation, not of the immortality of the soul but of "the resurrection of the flesh."[4] The differences between these two views, as expounded throughout Cullmann's book, are set out in the table below.

When we realize just how radically different the two doctrines are, we can understand Cullmann's suggestion that "for the Greeks who believed in the immortality of the soul it may have been harder

Immortality of the Soul	Resurrection of the Dead
The soul is imprisoned in the body.	The soul belongs in the body.
The body is inherently evil and so needs to be abandoned.	The body is inherently good yet corrupted by evil, and so needs to be redeemed.
Human death is a friend, a blessing; it is a natural passage from a lower to a higher form of life.	Human death is an enemy, a curse, the consequence of sin; it is a passage from life to a shady, incomplete state of existence.
All human beings irrespective of their beliefs or conduct inherently possess this immortality of the soul.	All human beings will be judged, and only those who are redeemed will receive immortal life (in the body).
A complete state of blessedness is attained immediately upon death.	A complete state of blessedness is attained only in the future resurrection from the dead.
Human immortality is based on universal human nature.	Human immortality is based on the particular death and resurrection of Jesus Christ, the divine Son incarnate.
Immortality involves passing from the material world to the immaterial world.	Immortality involves passing from this age to the age to come.

to accept the Christian preaching of the resurrection than it was for others."[5]

Got Soul?

Much of the argument over the state of the dead revolves around the word "soul." This English word regularly translates the Hebrew word *nephesh* in the Old Testament and the Greek word *psychē* in the New Testament. The long and the short of the matter is that these words have different meanings in different contexts. Any attempt to make either word into a technical term that always has the same meaning simply won't work.

Probably the most notable statement in the Old Testament using the word "soul" is this description of man's creation: "Then the LORD God formed man from the dust of the ground, and breathed into his nostrils the breath of life; and the man became a living being," that is, "a living *nephesh*" (Gen. 2:7). Here a human being is said to *be* a "soul," or to put it the other way around, the word "soul" (*nephesh*) here means a being. In this plain, biological sense of the word, any creature that breathes may be called a "soul," including animals (Gen. 1:30; cf. Rev. 8:9).

The Old Testament does not appear to use *nephesh* to refer to an immaterial aspect of human nature that exists after death, because what *nephesh* generally denotes is physical, biological life. This doesn't mean that the Old Testament views death as total extinction; it just means that it doesn't use the word *nephesh* to refer to what continues to exist after death.

There are, we should note, occasional statements suggesting that a person's *nephesh* is more than just his biological life. Especially in later, poetic writings of the Old Testament, the "soul" is sometimes something that one *has* (rather than something one *is*, as in Gen. 2:7) and that goes beyond the biological. The psalmist prays, "My soul thirsts for God, for the living God" (Ps. 42:2; cf. 63:1; 84:2; 119:20; 143:6). The term *nephesh* is occasionally used of God, perhaps as an idiomatic way of speaking (e.g., Lev. 26:11, 30; Isa. 1:14; 42:1), but also suggesting that the life of a *nephesh* can be spiritual as well as biological.

"The Soul Who Sins Will Die"

Another key passage using *nephesh* is Ezekiel 18. Here God tells Israel, "The soul who sins will die" (Ezek. 18:4, 20 NASB).[6] This is just one of many statements in the Old Testament that explicitly speaks about the soul dying. The word "soul" in the Old Testament, then, does not refer to something that cannot die. However, there is more to this passage than meets the eye. The context is God's standard of individual responsibility. The Israelites had a proverb:

> The fathers eat the sour grapes,
> But the children's teeth are set on edge. (Ezek. 18:2)

The point of this proverb was that children were often made to suffer the consequences of their parents' actions. God tells Israel through Ezekiel, "You are surely not going to use this proverb in Israel anymore" (v. 3).

The Lord goes on in Ezekiel 18:4: "Behold, all souls are Mine; the soul of the father as well as the soul of the son is Mine. The soul who sins will die." Each "soul," then, will die for his own sin, not for the sin of his parents (or of his children). We can take this statement in two ways — and perhaps both are meant. God could be telling Israel what standard of justice he expects them to uphold in their courts: children should not be punished for the offenses of their parents. Or God could be telling Israel what standard of justice he will uphold over all people: whatever Israel's legal system might do, God will judge each person as an individual and administer his own divine justice based on the principle of individual responsibility. As the passage unfolds, it becomes clearer that this latter understanding is precisely what God is saying.

Although "the soul who sins will die," the converse is also true: the soul who does not sin will *not* die: " 'But if a man is righteous and practices justice and righteousness ... [if] he walks in My statutes and My ordinances so as to deal faithfully — he is righteous and will surely live,' declares the Lord GOD" (Ezek. 18:5–9). If a righteous man has a wicked son, that son "will surely be put to death; his blood will be on his own head" (v. 13). But if the son observes "all his father's sins" and "does not do likewise ... he will not die for his father's iniquity; he will surely live," while the father "will die for his iniquity" (vv. 14–18).

> The person [*nephesh*] who sins will die. The son will not bear the punishment for his father's iniquity, nor will the father bear the punishment for the son's iniquity; the righteousness of the righteous will be upon himself, and the wickedness of the wicked will be upon himself. (v. 20)

So far, this standard of justice seems to be one that God expected Israel to administer. However, what God tells Israel next suggests that he is looking beyond legal justice to the ultimate Day of Judgment:

> But if the wicked man turns from all his sins which he has committed and observes all My statutes and practices justice and righteousness, he shall surely live; he shall not die. All his transgressions which he has committed will not be remembered against him; because of his righteousness which he has practiced, he will live. (Ezek. 18:21–22)

By contrast, the righteous man who turns to evil will die (v. 24). Although Israel rejected this standard of judgment, God insists that their ways are not right (vv. 25–29). He concludes:

> "Therefore I will judge you, O house of Israel, each according to his conduct," declares the Lord GOD. "Repent and turn away from all your transgressions, so that iniquity may not become a stumbling block to you. Cast away from you all your transgressions which you have committed and make yourselves a new heart and a new spirit! For why will you die, O house of Israel? For I have no pleasure in the death of anyone who dies," declares the Lord GOD. "Therefore, repent and live." (vv. 30–32)

By the end of the passage, then, God makes it clear that he will judge each individual and dispense justice even if Israel does not. The chapter looks beyond the administration of earthly justice to the final judgment on all humanity in which God promises to redress all injustices. Whatever may happen in this life, the wicked will eventually get what is coming to them, as will the righteous.

In this context God warns the wicked that they will "die" and assures the righteous that they will "live." If the soul who sins will die, the soul who does not sin — or who repents of sin — will not die. Thus, although the "soul" is mortal, in some sense it need not die. But this means that physical death does not necessarily bring about the death of the soul — since some souls are promised that they will not die. Ezekiel 18, then, while conflicting with the pagan doctrine of "the immortality of the soul," encourages the belief that the soul continues in some way to exist beyond physical death and can live forever.

"Unable to Kill the Soul"

The idea intimated in Ezekiel 18 is made explicit in the New Testament, in the teaching of Jesus himself. Two of the Gospels report Jesus' assertion that the death of the body does not mean the death of the soul.

> Do not fear those who kill the body but cannot kill the soul [psychē]; rather fear him who can destroy both soul [psychē] and body in hell [Gehenna]. (Matt. 10:28)

> I tell you, my friends, do not fear those who kill the body, and after that can do nothing more. But I will warn you whom to fear: fear him who, after he has killed, has authority to cast into hell [Gehenna]. Yes, I tell you, fear him! (Luke 12:4–5)

Once again, it is made explicit in Matthew that the soul is not immortal in the sense of being impervious to death; it can be killed or "destroyed." (We will comment below on what it means for the soul to be "destroyed.") However, as Jesus uses the word "soul" here, *human beings cannot kill another person's soul*. Killing the body does not result in the death of the soul. It survives — "lives," in some sense — after the death of the body. (Luke doesn't use the word "soul," leaving unspecified what exists after the body is killed, but his wording of Jesus' statement amounts to the same idea: something survives the death of the body that can then be "cast into hell" by God.)

The teaching that physical death means the extinction of the human person and the nonexistence of the soul entails that murderous human beings successfully kill one soul for each and every body that they kill. This follows logically from the claim that the soul is nothing but the biological life of the body. If that is what the soul is, then one cannot kill the body *without* also killing the soul. But Jesus says that murderous human beings can kill the body but *cannot* kill the soul. Therefore, the claim that the word "soul" always means merely the biological life of a human being is directly contradicted by Matthew 10:28.

Jehovah's Witnesses, recognizing the problem, attempt to finesse their way around this passage by asserting that what Jesus meant was that human beings can kill the body but they cannot kill the potential for the resurrection of the persons they kill. "By referring to the 'soul' separately, Jesus here emphasizes that God can destroy all of a person's life prospects; thus there is no hope of resurrection for him."[7] So now, according to the *Watchtower*, what Jesus meant in Matthew 10:28 was, "Do not fear those who can kill the body but cannot kill all of the life prospects, but rather fear him who can destroy both life prospects and body in Gehenna." Here Jehovah's Witnesses abandon their standard definition of 'soul' as the biological life of the body, implicitly conceding that it is not possible to maintain this definition in every occurrence.

Their explanation, however, amounts to definitional sleight-of-hand. There is no sound reason to explain "soul" (*psychē*) to mean a person's "life prospects" in the future resurrection. The word pair of "body" and "soul" (*sōma, psychē*) clearly refers to the outer and inner, or material and immaterial, aspects of an individual human being. This is how the Greek word pair was customarily understood by Jews as well as non-Jews, and this understanding comfortably fits the text before us.

Before leaving this saying of Jesus, we should comment on Jesus' statement that the soul can be "destroyed" in Gehenna. This statement may seem fatal to the view that the souls of the wicked will continue to exist in Gehenna (Hell). But it is not. The word "destroyed" (*apolesai*), a form of *apollymi*, need not and often does not mean "annihilated." Destruction is a relative concept; it can mean anything from annihilation to ruin. In the very same chapter in Matthew, the same verb is used to mean "to lose" (Matt. 10:42), and another form of the same verb is used to mean "lost" (v. 6). Jesus also speaks explicitly in the same chapter of the danger of "losing" one's soul: "The one who has found his soul will lose [*apolesei*] it, and the one who has lost [*apolesas*] his soul for my sake will find it" (v. 39, translation ours; see also 16:25).

The contrast with "finding" one's soul proves that *apollymi* here means to "lose" one's soul. So, when Jesus uses the same words (*apollymi* and *psyche*) together earlier in the same passage, we must consider the possibility that something other than extinction or annihilation is in view. Again, this doesn't mean they will be *alive*. The mere existence of the wicked in Hell cannot be called *life*; what awaits them there is *anti-life*, personal existence devoid of all that is good, that is characterized by utter ruin, waste, devastation, and loss.

A Balanced View of the Soul

Matthew 10:28 is not the only New Testament text that speaks of human beings as having a spiritual component or aspect that exists after the death of the body. The understanding that human beings have two aspects or dimensions to their being is found here and there in the New Testament and is especially clear in the writings of the apostle Paul.

Paul uses a variety of terms to refer to these two aspects of human nature. Once he speaks of humans as "body" and "spirit" (1 Cor. 7:34; see also James 2:26). A couple of times he speaks of humans as "flesh" and "spirit" (1 Cor. 5:5; 2 Cor. 7:1). In yet another word pairing, Paul speaks of a person's "outer man" and "inner man" (2 Cor. 4:16 NASB; cf. Eph. 3:16). Sometimes Paul uses more than one term for each aspect. For example, in Romans 7 Paul uses the terms "body" and "flesh" interchangeably for that aspect of him that wants to sin (vv. 18, 23–25), and the terms "inner man" and "mind" interchangeably for that aspect that wants to obey God (vv. 22–25 NASB). As we will see in the next chapter, Paul fully expected that when his body died, he would be spiritually present with Christ (2 Cor. 5:1–8; Phil. 1:21–23).

A sound understanding of death and what happens afterward, then, must avoid two extremes. On one end of the extreme is the pagan Greek doctrine of the immortality of the soul, according to which the soul is the inherently good part of a human being and needs to be released from the body in order to be fully alive. At the other extreme is the doctrine that the soul ceases to exist when the body dies because the soul is nothing but the biological life of the body. Neither of these positions is biblical.

Unfortunately, Christian theology has often described the soul as "immortal" as a way of expressing the biblical truth that the soul continues to exist in an immaterial, incorporeal state after death and before resurrection. This language is confusing and at least verbally contradicts the Bible (as in Ezek. 18:4, 20). It would be best, then, if orthodox Christians stopped using the expression "immortality of the soul" to describe their belief. Cullmann admirably strikes the balance between the two erroneous extremes:

> The New Testament certainly knows the difference between body and soul, or more precisely, between the inner and the outer man. This distinction does not, however, imply opposition, as if the one were by nature good, the other by nature bad.... Both belong together, both are created by God. The inner man without the outer has no proper, full existence. It requires a body. It can, to be sure, somehow lead a shady existence without the body, like the dead in Sheol according to the Old Testament, but that is not a *genuine life*. The contrast with the Greek soul is clear: it is precisely apart from the body that the Greek soul attains to full development of its life. According to the Christian view, however, it is the inner man's very nature which demands the body.[8]

SENSE

The soul is not inherently immune from death.

_____

NONSENSE

There is no soul that exists after the body dies.

Chapter 6

BETWEEN DEATH AND GLORY

When Christians die, they go to be with Christ — but that's not the end of the story.

We have seen that the Bible teaches neither that the human soul is inherently "immortal" (impervious to death) and is better off separated from the body nor that the human soul ceases to exist altogether when the body dies. A similar range of extremes to be avoided pertains specifically to what happens to Christians — genuine believers in Christ — after they die. One extreme position maintains that at death Christians are immediately glorified in Heaven and begin to enjoy immortal, eternal life in full. The other position holds that at death Christians cease to exist until the resurrection, when they will be re-created in glorious form.

Against these two extremes is the view that between their individual deaths and the future resurrection, Christians exist in an *intermediate state* — that is, a kind of existence that anticipates but stops short of their future glory. This doctrine is widely criticized in our day from a variety of perspectives. We have already answered some of the criticisms in the preceding chapters. Here we will look more directly at the issue and make a case for the belief in an intermediate state.

Paradise Delayed?

In Luke 23:43 Jesus promises the one thief on the cross, "Truly I tell you, today you will be with me in Paradise." As traditionally understood, this statement is not referring to a future resurrection from the dead, but to a spiritual state of repose immediately following death. Jesus does teach that a future resurrection will one day occur (see 20:34–36), but what he promises the thief is something that precedes that final salvation.

In Acts, Luke also reveals that Jesus will one day return to the earth to bring about the restoration promised in the Old Testament prophets (Acts 1:11; 3:19–21). His promise to the repentant criminal must, therefore, be understood as a promise of penultimate blessedness. He will be in Paradise, but the full realization and consummation of the salvation of the world is future. Luke thus presents Jesus as affirming an intermediate state for his followers in which they will be blessed with his presence while they await the resurrection.

Religious groups that dispute the reality of an intermediate state take a different approach to this text. The Adventists and Jehovah's Witnesses, for example, believe that the dead do not exist at all but will be resurrected (by which they mean re-created) at the end of the age. For these groups, the usual way around the implications of an intermediate state in Luke 23:43 is to punctuate the sentence differently. The sentence is usually punctuated as follows:

"Truly I tell you, Today you will be with me in Paradise."

Adventists and Jehovah's Witnesses, however, punctuate the sentence to read:

"Truly I tell you today, You will be with me in Paradise."

The significant difference here is whether one places a comma before or after the word "today." Disagreement about where to place a comma in an English translation is possible because, as Bruce Metzger (a leading scholar on the text of the Greek New Testament) points out, "the older Greek manuscripts lack punctuation and are written without divisions between words."[1] If the break goes *before* the word "today," then Jesus is saying that the thief will be with him in Paradise on that very day. If the break goes *after* the word "today," then Jesus is making no statement as to when the thief's being in Paradise will begin.

The key to resolving this disagreement is the expression "Truly I tell you," or more literally, "Amen I say to you." This expression is found in ancient literature only in the Gospels on the lips of Jesus or in later writings quoting Jesus. His use of *amēn* to introduce his sayings "is entirely different from its use in the OT, the early church, or anywhere else in Jewish literature."[2] The Gospels report that Jesus uses this expression seventy-five times,[3] always to introduce something he is saying. Unless Luke 23:43 is the only exception, this introductory formula always has a break immediately following it. That is, in every other instance, the words introduced by "Amen I say to you" form a separate statement.[4]

In an attempt to turn the evidence for this introductory formula "Amen I say to you" on its head, advocates of the alternate punctuation claim that "I say to you today" was a "Hebrew idiom" and that Jesus was using this idiom in Luke 23:43. E. W. Bullinger, a late nineteenth-century writer, is often quoted in support of this claim:

> "I say unto thee this day" was the common Hebrew idiom for emphasizing the occasion of making a solemn statement (see Deut. iv. 26, 39, 40; v. 1; vi. 6; vii. 11; viii. 1, 11, 19; ix. 3; x. 13; xi. 2, 8, 13, 26, 27, 28, 32; xiii. 18; xv. 5; xix. 9; xxvi. 3, 16, 18; xxvii. 1, 4, 10; xxviii. 1, 13, 14, 15; xxix. 12; xxx. 2, 8, 11, 15, 16, 18, 19; xxxii. 46).[5]

But simply looking up these passages and comparing them to Jesus' expression "Amen I say to you" ought to be enough to put to rest this frequently cited argument. Not one of the passages that Bullinger cites from Deuteronomy uses the word *amēn*—which, as we have pointed out, is the most distinctive feature of Jesus' introductory formula.

Perhaps more surprisingly, not one of those Deuteronomy texts has "I say"! The Greek word translated "I say" in Jesus' sayings is *legō*, which he uses not only in the seventy-five occurrences with *amēn* but also some seventy other times in the Gospels to introduce his statements. The Greek translation of Deuteronomy never uses *legō* at all. Nor does the Hebrew text of these Deuteronomy texts have the equivalent of "I say." How can a group of sayings that use neither

"Amen" nor "I say" be claimed to establish a common idiom reflected in Jesus' expression "Amen I say to you"? Moreover, if Luke 23:43 did use the word "today" with the introductory words "I say to you" (with or without "Amen"), it would be the *only such occurrence* in the Gospels. It seems clear that Jesus is not employing a familiar idiom.

What about those "I say unto thee this day" texts that Bullinger says are so common in Deuteronomy? It turns out that *none of them* actually says "I say unto thee this day." The closest, if one can even use that word, that Moses comes to saying "I say to you today" is his statement, "Hear, O Israel, the statutes and the ordinances which I am speaking [Gk. *lalō*] in your hearing on this day [Gk. *en tē hēmera tautē*]" (Deut. 5:1 NASB). The words "which I am speaking in your hearing on this day" are not an introductory expression and they do not include the words "I say" (*legō*), "to you," or "today" (*sēmeron*), not to mention "Amen" (*amēn*). The parallel is too weak even to be taken seriously.

The typical expression in the texts Bullinger cites to document this phantom idiom is "which I am commanding you today" (Deut. 4:40; 6:6; 7:11; 8:1, 11; 10:13; 11:8, 13, 27, 28; 13:18; 15:5; 19:9; 27:1, 4, 10; 28:1, 13, 14, 15; 30:2, 8, 11, 16; cf. 26:16). Moses also says that he, or Heaven and Earth, "witness against you today" (4:26; 8:19; 30:19; 32:46), and says, "I set before you today" (11:26, 32; 30:15). The other texts that Bullinger cites are even less relevant. How Bullinger could make such an assertion and support it with a long list of biblical references that simply do not say what he claimed is puzzling, to say the least. How so many people can take his assertion seriously is an even greater puzzle. Let this be a lesson: It is always a good idea actually to look up the biblical references cited to support a claim!

The other line of reasoning commonly used against the conventional understanding of Luke 23:43 focuses on the meaning of "Paradise." According to Jehovah's Witnesses, Paradise in this verse refers to the future divine kingdom over which Jesus will rule, since the repentant criminal asked Jesus to remember him when he came into that kingdom (v. 42). But this argument assumes that Jesus could not answer the man's request with something even greater than he had asked. The man asked Jesus to "remember" him; Jesus promises that he will be "with" him. The man asked Jesus for a favor when he came into his kingdom (whenever that might be); Jesus promises that he will be with him that very day. The man asked for a place in the future kingdom; Jesus promises him a place in the present Paradise.

That Paradise can be understood as a present, spiritual reality is evident from Paul's comment about his experience of being caught up "to the third heaven ... into Paradise" (2 Cor. 12:2–4). Paul here "locates" or equates Paradise with "the third heaven" (i.e., some sort of spiritual, heavenly realm).[6]

"To Depart and Be with Christ"

Although the revisionist punctuation of Luke 23:43 favored by Adventists and Jehovah's Witnesses does not fit the distinctive language of Jesus in that verse, at least it is a linguistically possible translation. We cannot say the same for the Jehovah's Witnesses' fractured rendering of Philippians 1:21–24 in their New World Translation (NWT), one of the most egregious examples of mistranslation in the entire version.[7]

The easiest way to begin explaining the problem is to set the NWT rendering of the passage alongside another modern version—virtually *any* version, since it's difficult to find any other version that does the same hatchet job on the passage.[8] You will want to refer to the table comparing the NRSV and NWT (and feel free to pull out a third version and compare all three).

Philippians 1:21–24 (NRSV)	Philippians 1:21–24 (NWT)
[21]For me, living is Christ and dying is gain. [22]If I am to live in the flesh, that means fruitful labor for me; and I do not know which I prefer. [23]I am hard pressed between the two: my desire is to depart and be with Christ, for that is far better; [24]but to remain in the flesh is more necessary for you.	[21]For in my case to live is Christ, and to die, gain. [22]Now if it be to live on in the flesh, this is a fruitage of my work—and yet which thing to select I do not make known. [23]I am under pressure from these two things; **but what** I do desire is **the releasing** and the being with Christ, for this, **to be sure,** is far better. [24]However, for me to remain in the flesh is more necessary on YOUR account.

Although verse 21 goes smoothly enough, already in verse 22 you can see a problem. When the NWT breaks out into awkward, wooden English (e.g., "this is a fruitage of my work"), chances are the translators had a theological reason to be uncomfortable with any smooth, natural translation. Paul's meaning is clearly that if he stays alive, that will mean more fruit from his work in the gospel ministry. Unfortunately, that is not at all clear in the NWT. The reason for the awkward wording comes in the next two verses.

Virtually all translations (and interpretations) of Paul's words "I am hard pressed between the two" understands those two things to have been mentioned already in verse 21 (living *or* dying) and again in verses 23–24 (departing and being with Christ *or* remaining in the flesh). Living (v. 21)—that is, "to live in the flesh" (v. 22) and "remaining in the flesh" (v. 24)—is better because it "means fruitful labor" for Paul (v. 22) and "is more necessary" for the church (v. 24). That's why "living is Christ": If he lives, it's all about working for Christ, producing fruit for Christ, and ministering to the body of Christ here in the flesh. But "dying" (v. 21)—that is, "to depart" (v. 23)—"is gain" (v. 21) for Paul personally; it "is far better" for him because he will "be with Christ" (v. 23). Paul is therefore contrasting his personal desire (to depart and be with Christ) with what the Philippian Christians need (for him to remain in the flesh).

Throughout the passage, then, Paul considers two possible situations: (1) that he will die ("depart"), or (2) that he will live. The latter, he explains, will be better for the believers to whom he will be able to continue ministering. The former, however, would be "gain" for him (v. 21) because if Paul dies, he will be "with Christ." This notion is incompatible with the Jehovah's Witnesses' doctrine that death is the extinction of the human person. So, the NWT, quite evidently to salvage that doctrine, has grossly mistranslated verse 23 (though there are oddities throughout verses 22–24). The translation of verse 23 in the NWT presents Paul as considering a *third* possibility, in addition to his dying or continuing to live: "I am under pressure from these two things; but what I do desire...." According to an appendix published in some editions of the NWT, this "third thing" is to be with Christ, not when he dies, but at

Christ's future return. This is what Jehovah's Witnesses claim Paul means by "the releasing and the being with Christ."[9]

In order to rewrite the passage to come up with this "third thing," the translators of the NWT have made several unjustifiable alterations to the text. The easiest to understand is their rendering of the Greek word *analysai* as "releasing." The usual, literal meaning of the word is either "to return" or "to depart"; the verb means "return" in its only other New Testament use (Luke 12:36).[10] However, Paul uses the noun related to this word as a euphemism for death in another epistle: "For I am already being poured out as a libation, and the time of my departure [*analyseōs*] has come" (2 Tim. 4:6). When the same author uses the verb form of this word in the context of speaking of the possibility of his own death, it is clear that the same euphemistic usage is at play.

Another bit of twisting that the NWT does to Philippians 1:23 may seem subtle but it makes a significant difference. In order to insinuate a third consideration beyond the apostle's own death or continuing life in the flesh, the NWT adds the little word "but" in the middle of the verse to separate the "two things" from what follows: "I am under pressure from these two things; *but* what I do desire is the releasing and the being with Christ." Will it surprise the reader to learn that there is no conjunction at this point in the Greek text and no linguistic basis for inserting an adversative conjunction here? There is one belonging to the previous clause (*de*, a common conjunction meaning "but" or "now"), which apparently the NWT translators decided to move over one clause to "fix" the verse.

Suffice it to say that there are good reasons why virtually every translation ever produced fails to construe Philippians 1:23 as referring to a third option besides Paul's dying or continuing to live. The passage is a clear, explicit affirmation that for a believer, death is a way of going to "be with Christ."

We should acknowledge, however, that Jehovah's Witnesses do have a point: Paul elsewhere is explicit that ultimately our living with Christ will follow his return and the resurrection of believers (1 Thess. 4:13–17). Here again, the blessing of being with Christ between one's death and resurrection is a temporary, partial blessing that anticipates a future blessing that will be eternal and total. Still, being with Christ was such a wonderful prospect that Paul could not help but consider that much better for him personally. As he said elsewhere:

> Therefore, being always of good courage, and knowing that while we are at home in the body we are absent from the Lord—for we walk by faith, not by sight—we are of good courage, I say, and prefer rather to be absent from the body and to be at home with the Lord. (2 Cor. 5:6–8 NASB)

In this New Testament vision of death as passage to a preferable existence "with Christ," "at home with the Lord," we can now talk seriously about *life* after death. It is not life in its fullness, but it *is* life, and in some ways a better life than the one we now have. How could it not be, if it is with Christ? Once again, Oscar Cullmann articulates the point with clarity:

> Here we find fear of a bodiless condition associated with firm confidence that even in this intermediate, transient condition no separation from Christ supervenes (among the powers which cannot separate us from the love of God in Christ is death—Romans 8:38).... Death is conquered. The inner man, divested of the body, is no longer alone; he does not lead the shadowy existence which the Jews expected and which cannot be described as life.... Although he still "sleeps" and still awaits the resurrection of the body, which alone will give him full life, the dead Christian *has* the Holy Spirit. Thus, even in this state, death has lost its terror, although it still exists.[11]

SENSE

The fullness of life awaits our future resurrection to glory.

NONSENSE

There is no anticipation of that life for believers after death.

Chapter 7

TOUCH ME
AND SEE

Jesus rose from the dead in a glorified, supernaturally empowered human body.

As we explained briefly in chapter 2, at the core of the Christian faith is the death and resurrection of Jesus Christ. However, these core facts, especially the resurrection of Christ, are widely disbelieved or misinterpreted today. For our purposes in this chapter, we will assume that the resurrection of Christ took place as the New Testament describes.[1] Here we will focus on the nature of the resurrection state, both for Jesus and for believers.

For many contemporary religious groups and individuals, resurrection means translation to a purely spiritual, heavenly state. The orthodox position, however, taught in the early church and still affirmed by most conservative and evangelical church bodies, is that resurrection means bringing human beings back to human life, though in a glorious, immortal condition. This issue is crucial for our beliefs about Heaven and the eternal state of the redeemed. Unfortunately, there is much disagreement—and confusion—over what the New Testament says on this subject.

Reinterpreting the Resurrection

Nearly all of the modern, alternative religions that profess to be Christian and Bible-based deny that Jesus came back to human, physical life from the dead. The idea that Jesus rose bodily from the grave is considered incompatible with his being exalted to Heaven. Some of these religions take the simple, if implausible, position that Jesus did not die at all. For example, while Islam acknowledges that Jesus was a great prophet, it rejects the idea of his dying on the cross for our sins, teaching that Jesus was not crucified at all but rather ascended directly to Heaven.[2] Mary Baker Eddy, the founder of Christian Science, taught that all death is an illusion. She explains the apparent death of Jesus by insisting he was hiding in the tomb when everyone else thought he was dead! "His disciples believed Jesus to be dead while he was hidden in the sepulcher, whereas he was alive."[3]

Many New Agers, while not necessarily denying that Jesus died, believe that death is merely a passage to another form of life, and that Jesus was an "ascended" master who "rose" to a higher level of consciousness. New Agers also sometimes interpret resurrection as a metaphor for spiritual transformation in the here and now. This approach is notable in *A Course in Miracles*, a New Age textbook that purports to have been "channeled" (dictated) by Jesus. The *Course* defines resurrection as "*a change of mind*" in which one views life, death, and the world in a completely different way. One "overcomes death" by realizing that physical life, the body, the material world, and therefore death itself are all illusory. Gloria and Kenneth Wapnick, widely regarded as leading expounders of the *Course*, explain: "*Resurrection*, thus, only means freedom from the belief that we actually exist within a body and are a body."[4]

Other religions agree that Jesus died but deny that he rose from the grave. The Unification Church teaches that Jesus' death accomplished only spiritual redemption, thus necessitating a physical redemption to be accomplished in the end times (by the "Lord of the Second Advent," identified as Rev. Sun Myung Moon). In keeping with this doctrine, the Unificationists hold that Jesus was raised spiritually but not physically: "He was no longer a man seen through physical eyes, because he was a being transcendent of time and space."[5]

Jehovah's Witnesses also interpret Jesus' resurrection as spiritual, though for different reasons. They believe that Jesus was resurrected with a "spirit body" fit for life in Heaven and will therefore not be returning bodily to the Earth. His "second coming" is actually a period of spiritual presence that began in 1914 and will end (presumably very soon!) with Armageddon. An "anointed class" numbering 144,000 (almost all of whom are already in place) will have the same kind of "spirit bodies" to live in Heaven. The rest of humanity (except for the very wicked) will be raised with physical bodies to live on a Paradise Earth separated from Heaven.[6]

Among skeptics and liberals, a growing consensus has been building that the earliest Christians believed that Jesus had "risen" in a spiritual sense and that his physical body remained dead and buried (if they concede it had been buried in the first place). The usual route by which this explanation is reached is to interpret Paul's view of the resurrection in this way and to dismiss the physical resurrection accounts of the Gospels as later legendary accretions.[7] If anyone doubts that this issue is directly related to the question of the nature of Heaven, consider the fact that Colleen McDannell and Bernhard Lang, in their book *Heaven: A History*, find it helpful to present this view. According to them, if Jesus' resurrection was simply a spiritual passage to Heaven, Jesus' followers would expect the same for themselves. According to McDannell and Lang, that was Paul's view:

> Like Jesus, dead Christians also leave their physical bodies in the dust. God will eventually provide the dead with a new and imperishable "spiritual" body. Paul's language does not imply the restoration of the physical human body. He probably was not familiar with the legendary reports of the empty tomb of Jesus. The physical body, Paul assumed, remained in the grave.[8]

A spiritual resurrection! For all their differences, it is remarkable that skeptics, liberals, New Agers, Jehovah's Witnesses, Christian Scientists, and Unificationists — a list by no means exhaustive — all agree that the earliest Christians (represented by the apostle Paul) believed that Jesus had spiritually risen to an exalted heavenly state and that the idea of a physical resurrection of Jesus' dead body was a later misunderstanding. We will look at this interpretation of Paul closely in the next chapter to see if there is anything to it. But first, let's review what the Gospels say about Jesus' resurrection.

"He Is Not Here; He Has Been Raised"

All four Gospels report that on the Sunday morning following Jesus' execution and burial in a rock tomb, some women followers went to the tomb and found the tomb open and the body of Jesus missing from the tomb (Matt. 28:1–7; Mark 16:1–8; Luke 24:1–10; John 20:1–2).[9] According to the Synoptic Gospels, one or two angels were there at the tomb and told the women, "He is not here; for he has been raised" (Matt. 28:6; Luke 24:6; "He has been raised; he is not here," Mark 16:6). This statement closely links the absence of Jesus' body from the tomb ("He is not here") with his resurrection ("He has been raised").

The natural understanding of this statement, especially in an ancient Jewish culture for which resurrection typically meant the bringing back to life of the whole person (body and soul), is that the dead body of Jesus came to life and thus was no longer in the tomb. This understanding of Jesus' resurrection is just as clear in the Gospel of Mark (widely thought to have been the first Gospel written) as in the other Synoptic Gospels, even though Mark does not include any accounts of Jesus' resurrection appearances.[10]

The other three Gospels do, of course, tell about various appearances of Jesus to his followers, and all three include information indicating that Jesus was a physical being. In Matthew, whose account is the least detailed, the women "took hold of his feet and worshiped him" (Matt. 28:9), which would be difficult if his feet were not solid. In Luke, Jesus assured his disciples, "See my hands and my feet, that it is I myself. Touch me, and see. For a spirit does not have flesh and bones as you see that I have" (Luke 24:39 ESV). Jesus then "showed them his hands and his feet" (v. 40) and ate "a piece of broiled fish" while they watched (vv. 41–43). Luke later quotes Peter commenting that he and the other apostles "ate and drank with him after he rose from the dead" (Acts 10:41).

In John's Gospel, two of the apostles visited the tomb, verified the body was not there, and observed the burial cloths in which the body had been wrapped left behind (John 20:4–7). Later, in a passage paralleling Luke's account in significant ways, Jesus appeared to his disciples and "showed them his hands and his side" (John 20:20). About a week later Jesus appeared to the disciples again, this time inviting Thomas, who had not been present the first time and who wanted to see and touch the marks left by his crucifixion on his body, to do so: "Reach here with your finger, and see My hands; and reach here your hand and put it into My side; and do not be unbelieving, but believing" (John 20:25–27 NASB).

No wonder that skeptics and liberals discount these elements of the Gospel accounts as later legendary embellishments. There are religious groups such as Jehovah's Witnesses, though, who acknowledge the reliability of the whole Bible, and yet who reject a physical resurrection of Jesus. According to them, "Jesus simply materialized or took on a fleshly body, as angels had done in the past," in order to convince his disciples that it was really him.[11] Thus, "by his repeatedly appearing to them in materialized bodies and then saying and doing things that they would identify with the Jesus they knew, he strengthened their faith in the fact that he truly had been resurrected from the dead."[12] In support of this explanation, the Witnesses argue that "Jesus did not always appear in the same body of flesh (perhaps to reinforce in their minds the fact that he was then a spirit), and so he was not immediately recognized even by his close associates."[13]

A careful reading of the texts that Jehovah's Witnesses cite from the Gospels to support their explanation shows otherwise. The only reference to Jesus' appearing in different bodies is Mark 16:12 ("He appeared in another form"), part of the so-called Long Ending of Mark, a passage almost universally recognized by biblical scholars as a later addition to the Gospel.[14]

In Luke, the two disciples who met Jesus on the road to Emmaus did not recognize him, not because he was in a different form or body, but because "their eyes were kept from recognizing him" (Luke 24:16). Just before he disappeared, "their eyes were opened, and they recognized him" (v. 31). In both passages the passive verbs "were kept" and "were opened" are examples of the "divine passive," a locution common in the New Testament using the passive to refer to actions done by God.[15] In other words, God kept the two men from recognizing Jesus right away—which implies that in the absence of this divine prevention they would have recognized Jesus with no problem.

The Gospel of John reports two occasions when someone did not immediately recognize Jesus, but neither of these supports the conclusion that he was appearing in a different body. Mary Magdalene mistook Jesus for the gardener; but John tells us that it was early in the morning, that she was crying, and that she was not looking directly at him (John 20:11–15). Under those conditions, it would have been surprising if Mary had recognized Jesus immediately. Later, when some of the disciples were out fishing on the Sea of Galilee, they saw Jesus standing on the shore but did not immediately recognize him (John 20:2–4). However, John tells us that it was daybreak and that they were two hundred cubits (about a hundred yards) out from the shore when they first saw him (20:4, 8)—about the length of a modern football field. Again, it would be surprising if they could identify him from that distance at early dawn.

Physical yet Supernatural

The Gospels report that Jesus' dead body was not in the tomb because he had risen, and that in his risen state he had a body with "flesh and bones" (Luke 24:39), hands and feet, and marks from his crucifixion—a body that could be touched and held by other people, that could eat and drink, and that his friends recognized him unless they were divinely prevented or were looking at him in dim light, through tears, or from far away. That the Gospels present Jesus as having been physically raised from the dead is therefore conceded by virtually all biblical scholars, including skeptics and liberals.

> That the Gospels present Jesus as having been physically raised from the dead is conceded by virtually all biblical scholars, including skeptics and liberals.

But the Gospel accounts of Jesus' appearances also suggest that he was more than an ordinary physical being. His sudden appearances and disappearances, even in rooms where the doors were locked, imply some sort of supernatural power (Luke 24:31, 36; John 20:19, 26). (The common assertion that Jesus "walked through walls" is incorrect; the texts state that he suddenly appeared in or disappeared from the room, not that he walked through a wall.) Jesus' ascension into Heaven, reported only by Luke (Luke 24:50–51; Acts 1:9–11), also obviously implies some sort of supernatural state.

That Jesus in his resurrected state was both physical and supernatural is the consistent view of the New Testament and the historic position of Christianity. Contrary to what skeptics, liberals, and various new religions assert, it was also the position of the apostle Paul, as we will see in the next chapter.

SENSE

Jesus rose from the dead in a physical, yet supernatural, body.

NONSENSE

Jesus rose from the dead but his body did not come back to life.

Chapter 8

O DEATH, WHERE IS YOUR STING?

When Jesus rose from the dead, he conquered death for us.

The question of the nature of the resurrection body of Jesus is important for our view of redemption and of Heaven itself because Jesus' resurrection is not an isolated occurrence. It is, in fact, the beginning of the resurrection of the dead for all of God's people. Our view of the nature of Jesus' resurrection, then, greatly affects our view of our own future resurrection, and vice versa.

The New Testament writer who most directly and thoroughly comments on the future resurrection of believers is the apostle Paul. It is commonplace today, even among many biblical scholars, to claim that Paul did not understand resurrection to mean the coming back to life of the human body.[1] As we will see, this common interpretation of Paul is mistaken.

"Will Give Life to Your Mortal Bodies"

Paul's most extended discussion of the subject of resurrection comes in 1 Corinthians 15, but he comments on the subject in several other places as well. He told the Philippians that Christ "will transform our lowly body that it may be conformed to His glorious body" (Phil. 3:21 NKJV). Here Paul speaks of the resurrection as a transformation of our present, lowly body, not as a replacement of that body with an entirely separate body. This transformation will make us fit for life in Heaven, as Paul has just said, "our citizenship is in heaven" (Phil. 3:20).

One of the more important passages in Paul's writings pertaining to resurrection occurs in Romans 8: "But if the Spirit of Him who raised Jesus from the dead dwells in you, He who raised Christ Jesus from the dead will also *give life to your mortal bodies* through His Spirit who dwells in you" (8:11 NASB). As the church father Augustine noted long ago, this statement "is a very explicit witness to the resurrection of the body."[2]

Most, if not all, New Testament occurrences of the Greek word translated "give life" (*zōopoieō*) are used in the context of resurrection (John 5:21; 6:63; 1 Cor. 15:22, 36, 45; Rom. 4:17; 2 Cor. 3:6; Eph. 2:6; Col. 2:12; 1 Pet. 3:18; possibly also Gal. 3:21). The parallel between the clauses "He who raised Christ Jesus from the dead" and "will also give life to your mortal bodies" proves that resurrection is meant in this text. The future tense used here ("will give life") points ahead to an event when our mortal bodies will be made alive (note the future tense verbs in vv. 13, 20–21, 32, 38–39). Throughout his epistles, Paul predicates our future resurrection on the resurrection of Jesus (Rom. 6:4–9; 1 Cor. 6:14; 15:12–23, 48–49; 2 Cor. 4:14; Phil. 3:10–11, 20–21; Col. 1:18; 2:12–13; 3:3–4; 1 Thess. 4:14), and he is doing that same thing here.[3]

For these reasons (and others that we will pass over here), virtually all commentators on Romans for nearly a century agree that Paul is speaking here of our future bodily resurrection. The view held by some older commentators that Paul was referring to a present sanctifying work of the Spirit in our bodies has now been almost universally abandoned.[4] Douglas Moo, in the most comprehensive commentary on Romans in the past half-century, puts it this way:

> Since reference to resurrection is so plain in the first part of the sentence, "will make alive" must also refer to future bodily transformation — through resurrection for dead believers — rather than, for instance, to spiritual vivification in justification, or to the "mortification" of sin in the Christian life.[5]

Paul goes on in the rest of Romans 8 to give a broader context for this idea of a future resurrection of our mortal bodies. We are, he says, God's children, and as such "joint heirs with Christ" who suffer now but one day will be glorified with him (Rom. 8:14–17). The whole creation is groaning in anticipation of that future glory, when "the creation itself also will be set free from its bondage to decay and obtain the freedom of the glory of the children of God" (v. 21 ESV). Paul envisions here, not the superseding of this creation with a different one, or the abandonment of the physical world for an immaterial Heaven, but the liberation of this creation from corruption. While creation groans with this anticipation, we do as well, waiting "for adoption as sons, the redemption of our bodies" (v. 23 ESV).[6] This is the Christian hope (vv. 24–25): full redemption, the redemption of soul (realized partially now) and body, of human beings and the creation in which we live.

The "Spiritual Body"

Those who deny that Paul believed in a resurrection of the human, dead body back to life usually make a controversial reading of 1 Corinthians 15 the primary basis for their argument.[7] Yet there is abundant evidence in this chapter supporting the traditional, orthodox Christian belief that Jesus rose in the same body in which he had died, albeit now glorified.

Paul begins his arguments against the Corinthian heretics by arguing for the truth of the bodily resurrection of Jesus from the dead. The sequence in 1 Corinthians 15:3b–5 is both chronological and logical:

> "that Christ *died* for our sins in accordance with the scriptures,
> and that he was *buried*,
> and that he was *raised* on the third day in accordance with the scriptures,
> and that he *appeared* to Cephas, then to the twelve." (1 Cor. 15:3b–5)

The mention of Christ's burial, coming between his death and resurrection, confirms that Jesus really had died and that he really left the tomb alive. As Anthony Thiselton in his recent, massive commentary notes, Paul's reference to Christ's burial *"underlines not only the reality of Christ's death but also the reality of his resurrection: had he not been **buried**, the genuine occurrence of either or both might lie more readily open to question."*[8] Any theory that denies the resurrection of the body that had been laid in the tomb negates Paul's argument. It was the Dead and Buried One who rose from the dead.

As we read through 1 Corinthians 15, it becomes clear that some church members in Corinth were troubled not so much by the idea of Christ's resurrection as by the idea that believers would also be raised from the dead. In response Paul makes several important points. He first argues that if, as some of these Corinthians were saying, dead people do not rise, then logically Christ could not have risen from the dead; and if that were the case, Christianity would be false, useless, and pitiful (1 Cor. 15:12–19). We aren't sure what exactly these Corinthians were thinking, denying a future resurrection while professing to follow a resurrected Christ, but that was apparently the situation. (Scholars' difficulty in coming up with a coherent account of what these Corinthians thought may be the result of their not *having* a coherent position!)

Paul then explains that Christ's resurrection was not an isolated occurrence or a special privilege granted to him alone, but the beginning of the restoration of the everlasting life forfeited by Adam (1 Cor. 15:20–22). The idea of Adam as a type of Christ—or, to put it the other way around, Christ as a latter-day, new Adam—is set out explicitly by Paul here and in Romans 5, and it is implicit throughout his epistles. Adam is the head of the human race in the original creation and in its fallen, sinful, mortal condition; Christ is the head of the redeemed human race, the new humanity, in the

BEN WITHERINGTON III

Paul's vision of the future, though involving a transformed condition called resurrection, definitely entails life on earth.... He looks forward to a new earth and new earthlings, not merely a new heaven.[9]

new creation (cf. Rom. 5:12–19; 6:4–11; 1 Cor. 15:20–22, 45–49; 2 Cor. 5:17; Gal. 6:15; Eph. 2:10, 15; 4:22, 24; Col. 1:18; 3:10). In this way also, Paul presents resurrection as the restoration and glorification of human beings, not as the abandonment of humanity for a purely ethereal existence in Heaven.

To the Greek mind, however, resurrection was impossible. As one Greek playwright put it, "Once a man has died, and the dust has soaked up his blood, there is no resurrection."[10] Given the corrupt nature of the human body and its mortality and weakness, the idea of resurrection seemed not only absurd but undesirable. This perspective on resurrection thus prompted some of the Corinthians to ask skeptical questions: "How are the dead raised? With what kind of body do they come?" (1 Cor. 15:35). Paul focuses on these concerns in his response, stressing the differences between the resurrection state and the mortal state. This focus and emphasis have been misconstrued by many as denying that the mortal body will be resurrected.

Paul begins his answers to the Corinthian skeptics by giving them three analogies for the resurrection from the physical creation. His first analogy is that of a seed and the full-grown plant that it becomes. "What you sow does not come to life unless it dies" (1 Cor. 15:36). Note that Paul states that what is sown does come to life, though it does so only after dying. In other words, that which is sown — here a metaphor for the mortal body (as Paul will make clear in vv. 42–44) — *will* come to life. To take Paul as meaning that the mortal body is not resurrected is a mistake.

In his second analogy, Paul points out that there are different kinds of flesh, such as the flesh of human beings, beasts, birds, and fish (1 Cor. 15:39). His point seems to be that since there can be different kinds of flesh, the resurrection of the body need not be a return to the condition or nature of our present mortal flesh. The Greeks were inclined to object to the resurrection of a person of flesh as if "flesh is flesh" and so any body of flesh will be plagued with the frailty and corruption we experience now. In rebuttal, Paul points out that there are different kinds of flesh, so God can resurrect human beings with a transformed nature that does not have the weaknesses of our present flesh.

Paul's third analogy notes that there are different kinds of bodies, including earthly and heavenly bodies, differing from one another in glory (1 Cor. 15:40). The earthly bodies probably refer to the different kinds of beings Paul has just mentioned in his previous analogies, while the heavenly bodies refer to the sun, moon, and stars (v. 41). This third analogy, then, ties together with the other two in making the point that resurrection need not mean a return to the lowly condition that presently characterizes human life.

"So also is the resurrection of the dead" (1 Cor. 15:42). With these words, Paul makes explicit that what he has been offering (vv. 36–41) were analogies and that he is now going to speak directly about the resurrection, drawing on those analogies to explain how the state of the resurrection will be different. He articulates four contrasts between the resurrection body and the mortal body (translating 15:42b–44a literally):

> "sown in corruption, raised in incorruption;
> sown in dishonor, raised in glory;
> sown in weakness, raised in power;
> sown a natural body, raised a spiritual body."

These four terse statements contrast the present, mortal body as corruptible, dishonorable, weak, and natural with the future, immortal resurrection body as incorruptible, glorious, powerful, and spiritual. If we are to understand the much-debated words "natural" and "spiritual" properly, we must see them in relation to the other words with which they are associated. That is, the "natural" body is corruptible, shameful, and weak; the "spiritual" body is incorruptible, glorious, and powerful.

For Paul, corruption is an aspect of the curse on humanity and on all creation from which we need to be redeemed (cf. Rom. 8:21). Paul will have more to say about corruption later in the chapter (1 Cor. 15:50–54). The "dishonor" or shame of our present condition likewise contrasts with the "glory" to be realized fully in the resurrection—a glory anticipated now as Christians "glorify God in [their] body" (6:20; cf. 2 Cor. 3:18).

Similarly, "weakness" (a word that in some contexts refers to sickness or other overt bodily infirmity) characterizes the present human condition from which Christ came to save us (e.g., Rom. 5:6) through the "power" of his resurrection (Rom. 1:4; 2 Cor. 13:4; Eph. 1:19–20; Phil. 3:10, 21). The point of these contrasts is not to contrast the physical with the nonphysical, the material with the immaterial. Rather, Paul is contrasting the fallen, unredeemed, present condition of our bodies (and our lives generally) with their raised, redeemed, future condition.

What, then, about the fourth contrast, between the "natural body" and the "spiritual body"? The word we have translated "natural" (*psychikos*) is erroneously translated "physical" in the NRSV (as well as in the New World Translation, published by Jehovah's Witnesses). This word is used elsewhere in the New Testament as a pejorative term for people living like animals, following their "natural" inclinations. James contrasts God's heavenly wisdom with the worldly kind that is "earthly, natural [*psychikos*], demonic" (James 3:15 NASB). Jude describes the false teachers he censures as "divisive, natural [*psychikos*], not having the Spirit" (Jude 19). In these passages the NRSV translates *psychikos* as "unspiritual" (James 3:15) and "worldly" (Jude 19 NASB); other translations use "sensual" in both texts (e.g., KJV, NKJV). These examples show that the word does not necessarily denote physicality; perhaps we could say that it refers to that which is *merely* physical, that which is governed only by physical desires or values.

The most important occurrence of the word *psychikos* for our purposes is earlier in the same letter of 1 Corinthians, where Paul again contrasts it with *pneumatikos* ("spiritual"):

> But a natural man [*psychikos anthrōpos*] does not accept the things of the Spirit of God, for they are foolishness to him; and he cannot understand them, because they are spiritually appraised. But he who is spiritual [*ho pneumatikos*] appraises all things, yet he himself is appraised by no one. (1 Cor. 2:14–15 NASB)

This contrast between "natural" and "spiritual" is not between the material and the immaterial, but between human beings dominated by the material and human beings illuminated by the Spirit. "The natural man" is a human being (*anthrōpos*), but so is "the one who is spiritual." Hence, the NRSV reads "those who are unspiritual" rather than "the physical human being," as one might have expected from its rendering of the same word in 1 Corinthians 15.

A "natural body," then, is one that remains unredeemed, that is still mortal, decaying, shameful, and weak. A "spiritual body" is one that as a result of the work of God's Spirit will be incorruptible, glorious, and powerful. The natural body is a *merely* physical, *merely* biological body, one that frustrates God's purposes for us because of its physical degradation and mortality and its tendency to corrupt us morally, to drag us down to base, materialistic, sensual, or worldly desires. The spiritual body will perfectly realize God's purposes for us because in it we will fully exhibit the power of the Spirit with immortality, incorruption, and perfect goodness.

The notion that the "spiritual" body will be spiritual in composition—that it will be composed of spirit, an immaterial substance akin to that of angels—has no basis in the text. None of the four contrasts in 1 Corinthians 15:42–44 has anything to do with whether the resurrection body will be material or immaterial.

Those who are merely "natural" people (1 Cor. 2:14 NASB), for whom caring for their "natural body" is all they care about, have as the head of their humanity the first Adam. Those who are "spiritual" people (2:14–15) and who look forward to having a "spiritual body" (15:44) have as the head of their humanity Christ, the last Adam. Adam was a mere "soul," a human being with merely natural life; Christ in his resurrection has become a life-giving "spirit" (15:45 NASB). Paul's contrast between the two Adams here is a contrast between *two men*, not between a man and an angel or other immaterial being. Paul says so explicitly: "The first man is from the earth, earthy; the second man is from heaven" (15:47 NASB).

The word "spirit" (*pneuma*) should be understood in this context, and the contrast between "soul" and "spirit" should be understood in light of the preceding contrast between the "natural" (*psychikos*, an adjectival form of *psychē*, "soul") and "spiritual" bodies. Christ is a man whose life is not merely biological or natural but is supernatural, empowered by the Spirit, and fit for life in the realm of the Spirit—for heavenly life. Hence whereas Adam, the first man, was from the earth and his life was merely earthly, Christ, "the second man," is "from heaven"; he is "the heavenly" man (1 Cor. 15:47–49). Adam was merely "of dust," in a form susceptible as a result of the fall to corruption and death (cf. v. 47). The resurrection and exaltation of Christ assures us that when Christ returns "from heaven," we will be raised and exalted to share in his heavenly image (vv. 47–49).

Paul now concludes his discussion of the resurrection: "Now I say this, brethren, that flesh and blood cannot inherit the kingdom of God; nor does the perishable inherit the imperishable" (1 Cor. 15:50 NASB). By now we ought to understand how Paul is speaking. He does not mean that biological people cannot inherit God's kingdom, but that *merely* biological, merely "flesh and blood," mortal people, cannot inherit eternal life in God's kingdom. The problem with flesh and blood people is not that they are material but, as he says in the rest of the sentence, that they are "perishable" or corruptible (the same word as in v. 42). The solution is not to become incorporeal or immaterial beings but to have the effects of sin reversed, being redeemed from corruption. Hence Paul concludes, "For this perishable must put on the imperishable, and this mortal must put on immortality" (v. 53 NASB). Our perishable or corruptible, mortal bodies are not to be discarded or abandoned to the dust, but they will be redeemed; they will *put on* incorruption and immortality.

Paul's view of resurrection in 1 Corinthians 15, then, is not in conflict with the understanding of resurrection reflected in the Gospel accounts—let alone in Paul's other writings. He too held that Christ was raised from the dead in the same body that had died and been buried. He too held that Christ's resurrection body was still that of a human. And he also held that Christ's resurrection body was glorious, supernatural, immortal, and capable of life in Heaven as well as life on Earth. This is, after all, the consistent teaching of the New Testament.

SENSE

Believers, like Christ, will be raised to glorious, immortal life.

NONSENSE

Resurrection means translation to a nonhuman form of life.

Chapter 9

THE BAD NEWS BEARS REPEATING

Hard as it may be to accept, not everyone is going to make it.

Polls consistently report that the vast majority of Americans believes in Heaven and a majority also believes in Hell. Not surprisingly, nearly everyone who professes to be a Christian affirms the reality of Heaven. What is somewhat surprising in our live-and-let-live, permissive culture is that about four-fifths of these American Christians, including both the theologically conservative and liberal, also affirm the reality of Hell. Even more surprising is that reportedly two-fifths of Americans who do not even consider themselves Christians also affirm that Hell exists. Of course, most of them do not expect to go there—although a few apparently do.[1]

Actually, the range of beliefs about Hell is much more varied and complex. There are plenty of opinions, even among those professing faith in Christ, as to what will happen to the wicked or unrighteous. Here are just some of those views:

- They will suffer everlasting punishment.
- They will suffer temporal punishment, and then be annihilated.
- They will simply be annihilated.
- They will suffer temporal punishment, and then some will be saved.

- They will suffer temporal punishment and then all will be saved.
- They will not suffer any punishment, but all will be saved.[2]

The last two options mentioned above are known as *universalism*—the belief that everyone will eventually be saved. We have in mind here the doctrine sometimes called Christian universalism, according to which Jesus Christ's death on the cross procured salvation for absolutely everyone whether they come to recognize it in this life or not. We are therefore setting aside the pluralist form of universalism, which maintains that all religions are paths to reconciliation to God, since this view cannot claim to be consistent with the teaching of the Bible.[3]

Universalism has been a distinctly minority view in the history of Christian thought.[4] This fact doesn't prove it false, but it does put the burden of proof on universalists. Polycarp, Ignatius, Justin Martyr, Theophilus of Antioch, Irenaeus, and Tertullian are some of the better-known Christians of the second century who believed in eternal judgment for the wicked. Universalism first arose in the third century in Alexandria, where Origen (c. 185–254) advocated a form of universalism.[5] The only other significant Christian universalist of the first four centuries appears to have been Gregory of Nyssa (c. 335–394). Universalism almost disappeared after him, although Maximus the Confessor (c. 580–662) taught a form of the doctrine.[6] The heyday of universalism came in the eighteenth and nineteenth centuries, though it enjoys significant support today.[7]

We should mention that there are a number of different kinds of Christian universalism. For example, all universalists agree that God will eventually save all human beings, but they disagree as to whether God will also save Satan and all his demonic followers. A moderate form of universalism holds that everyone *might* end up being saved, but we don't know that for sure. This moderate universalism typically views the biblical warnings about Hell as warnings about a possibility that (the universalist hopes) will not become an actuality. For our purposes, we will define Christian universalism as the belief that through the redemptive work of Jesus Christ, all human beings throughout history will be saved.

The Case for Universalism

The case for Christian universalism primarily rests on deductions from certain biblical doctrines that are thought to entail that everyone will be saved. There are two important arguments to consider here.

(1) Universalists reason that because God is all-loving, he would *want* to save everyone if he *could*, and because he is all-powerful and all-knowing, he *could* save everyone if he *wanted*; therefore, God surely will find a way to save everyone. We may call this "the argument from God's nature." Those with some background in philosophy of religion will recognize this argument as conceptually parallel to the so-called problem of evil: If God is all-powerful, he *could* stop all evil from happening, and if God is all-loving he would *want* to stop all evil from happening, so why hasn't he done so? Both arguments make a number of assumptions (e.g., that we know what God's love motivates him to want to do) that are (as we will see) biblically unjustifiable as well as question-begging.

(2) Universalists argue that God did find a way to save everyone. According to universalism, Jesus' redeeming death on the cross atoned for the sins of every human being, and therefore everyone will be saved. This argument, which we may call "the argument from Christ's atonement," also makes a number of assumptions—for example, that Christ's death was intended to procure salvation for every human being, an assumption that can be challenged biblically.

We agree that in a broad, general sense, Christ died to provide an atoning sacrifice sufficient to cover every sin of every person; his death was certainly enough to pay for the sins of anyone and everyone who believes in him. In that sense there is no limit to the saving power of Christ's redeeming blood. However, even Christian universalists agree that to be saved an individual must respond to God's grace. From this perspective, the atonement is limited or effective in saving only those who repent and receive God's mercy. In a specific sense, then, as the New Testament repeatedly states, Christ died not with the expectation of saving the whole world but only those whom the Father gave him to be his "sheep," his people, and his atoning death actually procures salvation only for them (see Matt. 1:21; John 10:11–16; 17:9, 20; Acts 20:28; Rom. 5:8; 1 Cor. 15:3; Eph. 5:25–27; Titus 2:14; Rev. 5:9).

Universalists cite a battery of proof texts from the Bible to support their deductive arguments. Most of these texts speak of "all" people or of "the world" as the object of God's love or saving work. Several texts are quoted to prove that God wants to save everyone. John writes that God sent his Son because he "so loved the world" (John 3:16). Paul says that God "desires everyone to be saved and to come to the knowledge of the truth" (1 Tim. 2:4), and Peter says that God is "not wanting any to perish, but all to come to repentance" (2 Pet. 3:9).

Moreover, universalists cite a larger number of texts in an attempt to show that God is accomplishing this objective through Christ. John the Baptist hails Jesus as "the Lamb of God who takes away the sin of the world" (John 1:29), and later some Samaritans confessed that Jesus was "the Savior of the world" (John 4:42). Jesus states that when he is "lifted up," he "will draw all people to myself" (John 12:32). In his first epistle, John states that Jesus Christ "is the propitiation for our sins, and not for ours only, but also for the whole world" (1 John 2:2 NKJV).

Paul states that through Christ's death "came righteousness leading to life for all people" (Rom. 5:18 NET). Later he says that "God has imprisoned all in disobedience so that he may be merciful to all" (11:32). Elsewhere he writes, "For as in Adam all die, so also in Christ all will be made alive" (1 Cor. 15:22 NASB), that "in Christ God was reconciling the world to himself" (2 Cor. 5:19), that one day "every tongue will confess that Jesus Christ is Lord, to the glory of God the Father" (Phil. 2:11 NASB), that it was God's good pleasure through Christ "to reconcile to himself all things" (Col. 1:19–20), that Christ "gave himself a ransom for all" (1 Tim. 2:6), and that God "is the Savior of all people, especially of those who believe" (4:10).

In response to these appeals to Scripture to prove universalism, we make three observations. (1) In many of these passages it is demonstrable from the immediate context that universal salvation is not being taught. John 3:16 does say that God loved the world, but it does not say that the world will not perish, but that "whoever believes in Him [the Son] shall not perish" (NASB). Peter's statement about God's not wishing for any to perish (2 Pet. 3:9) comes on the heels of his warning that a fiery "day of judgment and destruction" is coming for "the ungodly" (v. 7). Jesus made his comment about drawing all people to himself (John 12:32) shortly after saying, "Whoever loves his life loses it, and whoever hates his life in this world will keep it for eternal life" (v. 25 ESV).

The statement that through Christ's death "came righteousness leading to life for all people" (Rom. 5:18 NET) is qualified by the immediately preceding statement that "those who receive" this gift will "reign in life through the one, Jesus Christ" (v. 17 NET). When Paul says that "in Christ God was reconciling the world to himself" (2 Cor. 5:19), we know that he did not mean that every person in the world would be reconciled because the apostle immediately says that his ministry consisted of entreating people "on behalf of Christ, be reconciled to God" (v. 20).

(2) Close attention to the wording and background of these statements often shows that they are actually contradictory to the notion of universal salvation. Take, for example, Paul's statement, "For as in Adam all die, so also in Christ all will be made alive" (1 Cor. 15:22 NASB). Universalists misread this to say that because of Christ, everyone will be made alive. Paul is here contrasting what happens to all who are "in Adam" (they "die") with what happens to all who are "in Christ" (they "will be made alive"). He does not say, nor does he mean, that absolutely everyone is now or ever will be "in Christ." The people who are "in Christ" are those "who have hoped in Christ in this life" (v. 19), some of whom have "fallen asleep in Christ" (v. 18), and through their faith they are "those who are Christ's" (v. 23 [all NASB]).

Paul's statement that "every knee should bend ... and every tongue should confess that Jesus Christ is Lord, to the glory of God the Father" (Phil. 2:10–11) is an allusion to Isaiah 45:23, where the Lord says, "To me every knee shall bow, every tongue shall swear." In context, Isaiah is not teaching universal salvation, because he goes on immediately to contrast those who "will be put to shame" with those who "will be justified and will glory" in the Lord (45:24–25 NASB). Paul understood the text in this way, too, since he quotes it in Romans and then comments, not that everyone will be saved, but that "each one of us will be accountable to God" (Rom. 14:11–12).

(3) The words "all" and "world" are not necessarily references to every single individual human being in history. We have already seen that in some contexts "all" does not mean all human beings but rather all human beings "in Christ" (1 Cor. 15:22), all those who "receive" the gift of salvation through Christ (Rom. 5:17–18). The words "all" and "world" can be used in a variety of contexts, to which the universalistic interpretation is not sufficiently sensitive. For example, the "all" who have been imprisoned in disobedience and are being shown mercy (Rom. 11:32) are not all persons but all nations or peoples, both Jews (Israel) and non-Jews (Gentiles) of all types (Rom. 11:25–32).[8]

The statements in John's writings about Christ's saving, sacrificial death being for "the world" are best understood to be speaking in broad terms about the scope of those who will be redeemed in Christ being worldwide, including people from all nations and not just Jewish believers. Thus, John the Baptist's statement (John 1:29) contrasts with the religious parochialism of the Jewish leaders (vv. 19–28); the Samaritans' confession of Jesus as "Savior of the world" (4:42) highlights Jesus' willingness to go outside the Jewish people with his gospel; and presumably John's similar statements in 1 John 2:2; 4:14 reflect the same perspective.

The Case against Universalism

The case against Christian universalism is based on a mass of biblical texts, especially in the New Testament, that approach the subject from a variety of angles. We will consider just a few of the more explicit passages in the Gospels, using them to illustrate the way universalists misconstrue Scripture to support their position.

(1) *The easy road to destruction.* Jesus made one statement — reported in two of the Gospels in somewhat different settings —

that clearly indicates that not everyone is going to make it. In fact, these texts appear to limit the number of people who will be saved to a minority of the human race:

> Enter through the narrow gate; for the gate is wide and the road is easy that leads to destruction, and there are many who take it. For the gate is narrow and the road is hard that leads to life, and there are few who find it. (Matt. 7:13–14)

In Luke, a shorter version of this saying follows a question from Jesus' disciples: "Lord, will only a few be saved?" (Luke 13:23). Jesus' answer is, "Strive to enter through the narrow door; for many, I tell you, will try to enter and will not be able" (v. 24).

Now, in Luke one might make a case that Jesus is only saying that the number of those lost will be "many" without addressing the question of how that "many" compares numerically to the number of those saved. But in Matthew, Jesus' saying contrasts those who will find destruction as "many" with those who will find life as "few" (Matt. 7:13–14). This statement seems to entail that the number of people lost will be greater than the number of people saved.[9]

What is really beyond reasonable doubt is that Jesus teaches in these passages that not everyone will find the gate or path to life. Universalists must read into these passages the idea that many people won't find the way to life *before they die* but that everyone who misses it in this life will find it sometime after they die. But Jesus is not contrasting those who find the way in this life with those who find it in the next; rather, he is contrasting those who find the way to life with those who take the way to destruction. The contrast as stated is meaningless if everyone will find the way to life eventually. In context, Jesus goes on to warn his followers that not everyone "will enter the kingdom of heaven" and that he will tell "many" who claim to be his followers, "Go away from me" (Matt. 7:21–23).

(2) *Unforgivable sin.* After Jesus casts a demon out of a man, his religious opponents accuse him of being a stooge of Satan — in effect being in league with the Devil to stage the exorcism. Jesus condemns their lie in the strongest possible terms.

> Therefore I tell you, people will be forgiven for every sin and blasphemy, but blasphemy against the Spirit will not be forgiven. Whoever speaks a word against the Son of Man will be forgiven, but whoever speaks against the Holy Spirit will not be forgiven, either in this age or in the age to come. (Matt. 12:31–32)

Jesus explicitly contrasts sins that "will be forgiven" with a sin that "will not be forgiven." Some universalists argue that this contrast reflects a Hebrew idiomatic way of speaking that means merely that the one sin will be much more difficult to get forgiven than the others. To illustrate this idiom, they quote Jesus' statement, "Heaven and earth will pass away, but my words will not pass away" (Matt. 24:35), which they argue "does not mean that heaven and earth shall actually pass away, but they will sooner fail than his words. It is a strong method of asserting that his words shall be fulfilled."[10]

This comparison is confused. If the two passages are using the same idiom, shouldn't Matthew 12:32 mean that other sins will not actually be forgiven while the sin of blaspheming the Holy Spirit definitely will not be forgiven? Let's assume for the sake of argument that "Heaven and earth will pass away, but my words will not pass away" (Matt. 24:35) means that heaven and earth will sooner pass away than Jesus' words pass away. If Matthew 12 uses the same idiom, then "Whoever speaks a word against the Son of Man will be forgiven, but whoever speaks against the Holy Spirit will not be forgiven" (Matt. 12:32) means that the one speaking against the Son of Man will sooner be forgiven than the one speaking against the Holy Spirit is forgiven. That doesn't seem to help the universalist position at all.

(3) *Better never to have been born.* At the Last Supper, Jesus had this to say about Judas Iscariot: "Woe to that one by whom the Son

JOHN BLANCHARD

All the ways to hell are one-way streets. The idea that those who go there will eventually be released and join the rest of humanity in heaven has not a shred of biblical evidence to support it.[11]

of Man is betrayed! It would have been better for that one not to have been born" (Matt. 26:24; Mark 14:21). J. I. Packer comments: "Universalism, however, must respectfully decline to endorse Jesus' judgment here, at least in its obvious meaning, since they themselves expect Judas to be saved."[12] Indeed so. Universalists sometimes compare Jesus' warning here to Job's lament that he was ever born (Job 3:3). It is difficult to take this comparison seriously: Job was complaining bitterly and hyperbolically in a poem of lament, whereas Jesus is issuing a chilling prophetic pronouncement of "woe" to his betrayer.

(4) *Eternal punishment.* At the end of his parable of the sheep and the goats, Jesus said, "These [the goats] will go away into eternal punishment, but the righteous into eternal life" (Matt. 25:46). Universalists have spilled a great deal of ink (and today fill a great deal of cyberspace) arguing that the Greek word *aiōnion* should be translated neither as "eternal" nor as "everlasting." They point out, correctly, that in some contexts the word means "of perpetual or indefinite duration," rather than strictly forever. Since the word is an adjectival form of the noun *aiōn*, meaning "age," they argue that *aiōnion* means something like "age-enduring," "age-lasting," or "of the age (to come)."[13] They conclude that in 25:46 Jesus is promising that his faithful followers will enjoy life in the coming age whereas the wicked will suffer punishment in the same coming age. They then suggest that this coming "punishment" will be corrective or chastening in purpose, so that those so punished will eventually repent and be saved.

The universalist argument gets the color of the bark correct but misclassifies the tree. In a covenantal or legal context *aiōnion* meant something like our legal phrase "in perpetuity," usually in the term "perpetual covenant" or "perpetual statute." A majority of its occurrences in the Greek Old Testament, most of which are in the legal sections of the Pentateuch, fall into this category.[14] The word is also used about a dozen times hyperbolically in translating Hebrew poetry in such expressions as "ancient paths" or "everlasting hills."[15] In other contexts, though, it does mean "eternal" or "everlasting," as when it is used to describe God ("Everlasting God," Gen. 21:33; Isa. 26:4; 40:28).

Of more direct relevance is the use of *aiōnion* in contexts dealing with God's future plans for humanity (what scholars call an *eschatological*, or last things, context). For example, Isaiah looks forward to a future time when Israel will be saved "with an everlasting salvation" and will not be ashamed "to all eternity" (lit., "unto the age," Isa. 45:17). The Lord promises that he will be his people's "everlasting light" (60:19, 20; 61:7). According to Jeremiah, by contrast, the false prophets who lied to Jerusalem will suffer "everlasting disgrace and perpetual shame, which shall not be forgotten" (Jer. 23:40). Daniel speaks of the Son of Man's "everlasting" dominion and kingdom that "shall not pass away" (Dan. 7:14, 27). The prophet looks forward to the establishment of "everlasting righteousness" (9:24). The climax of Daniel's prophecies uses the same word to describe the futures awaiting those who have died:

> Many of those who sleep in the dust of the earth shall awake, some to *everlasting life*, and some to shame and *everlasting contempt*. Those who are wise shall shine like the brightness of the sky, and those who lead many to righteousness, like the stars forever and ever [*eis ton aiōna tou aiōnos*, unto the age of the age]. (Dan. 12:2–3)

The reader should notice a couple of important points about this passage. (a) The eschatological context of the future resurrection and the earlier uses of *aiōnion* in the Greek translation of Daniel make it clear that the word here means "everlasting" or "eternal," not merely "perpetual" or for an indefinite period of time. This conclusion is confirmed by the closing emphatic phrase "unto the age of the age," which in English is normally and properly translated "forever and ever."

(b) Jesus' statement in Matthew 25:46 clearly echoes this text. Daniel says that some will be raised to "everlasting life" while others will be raised to "everlasting contempt." The Judge who determines who will receive which of these futures is "the Son of Man" when he "comes in his glory" to judge "all the nations" (25:31–32), whom the book of Daniel says will have "everlasting" glory, authority, and kingdom over "all the nations" (Dan. 7:14, 27).

Once we understand the specific way in which the word *aiōnion* is used in biblical prophetic speech pertaining to the future of all humanity and especially the way Jesus' statements hearken back to Daniel, it is clear that "*aiōnion* punishment" means "everlasting punishment"—the disgrace, contempt, and shame that will come on the unredeemed in the age to come. In biblical thought, the time for repenting, believing, and turning to God is in this age; in the age to come, it will be too late.

SENSE

Salvation is available to "whoever will."

NONSENSE

Everyone "will."

Chapter 10

JUST DON'T GO THERE!

Jesus led the way in teaching that wicked angels and people would go to Hell.

In the previous chapter we established that not everyone will be saved. Some people simply will not enjoy eternal life in God's presence. In making the case against universalism, we have already seen some of the evidence for the doctrine of eternal punishment, but we have not demonstrated just what that means. Many people today find the very idea of Hell offensive and assume it was invented by church leaders to "keep the people in line."

The first step in understanding what the Bible teaches about Hell is to read what it says. In this chapter we will survey the major New Testament passages related in some way to Hell. Our goal here is not to draw doctrinal conclusions but to get the lay of the land. We will see that belief in Hell was not an invention of the church but the teaching of Jesus and his apostles.

Gehenna: The Fiery Hell

All but one reference to *Gehenna* (the one biblical word properly translated "hell") in the New Testament comes from Jesus in the Synoptic Gospels. In response to the rabbinical view that murderers were liable to the court, Jesus says that "everyone who is angry with his brother" or insults him will be liable to the court, "and if you say, 'You fool,' you will be liable to the hell of fire" (Matt. 5:21–22). Jesus goes on to warn his listeners to resolve disputes with their fellow believers or face the possibility of being "thrown into prison," where they will remain until they have "paid the last penny" (5:25–26; see also Luke 12:58–59).

This warning seems to be referring to Hell, since Jesus goes on to warn that if your eye or hand causes you to stumble into sin, it would be better "to lose one of your members than for your whole body to be thrown into hell" (Matt. 5:29; "to go into hell," v. 30). A similar idea appears at the end of Jesus' parable about an unforgiving servant: "And in anger his lord handed him over to be tortured until he would pay his entire debt" (18:34). In case it isn't clear that the parable is referring to Hell, Jesus even states explicitly that his heavenly Father will do the same to those who don't forgive their brothers (v. 35).

Jesus makes other statements about giving up body parts rather than going to Hell. "It is better for you to enter life with one eye, than to have two eyes and be thrown into the hell of fire" (Matt. 18:9). Or again, after Jesus warned that anyone who causes one of his "little ones" to stumble would be better off thrown into the sea with a millstone around his neck, he goes on: If your hand causes you to stumble in sin, it would be better to cut it off and "enter life maimed" than to keep your hands but "go into hell, into the unquenchable fire." Likewise, it would be better "to enter life lame than ... to be thrown into hell" (Mark 9:42–45). Jesus concludes this series of warnings with an even more graphic warning: It would be better "to enter the kingdom of God with one eye than ... be thrown into hell, where 'their worm does not die, and the fire is not quenched'" (9:47–48 NIV).

In parallel passages we discussed earlier (ch. 5), Jesus urges his followers not to fear people, because they can only kill their bodies. Rather, he says, they should "fear him who can destroy both soul

JESUS CHRIST

Depart from Me, accursed ones, into the eternal fire which has been prepared for the devil and his angels. (Matt. 25:41 NASB)

and body in hell" (Matt. 10:28), or, as it is worded in Luke, "fear him who, after he has killed, has authority to cast into hell. Yes, I tell you, fear him!" (Luke 12:5). In Jesus' harshest denunciation of the Pharisees, he describes a Pharisee convert as "twice as much a child of hell as yourselves" and asks rhetorically, "How can you escape being sentenced to hell?" (Matt. 23:15, 33).

Finally, James has an interesting reference to Gehenna. He writes, "The tongue is a fire" that enflames the course of a person's life and "is itself set on fire by hell" (James 3:6).

An Eternal Fire Fit for the Devil

In the same context as a statement quoted earlier about being "thrown into the hell of fire" (Matt. 18:9), Jesus warns that it is better "to enter life maimed or lame, than ... to be thrown into the eternal fire" (v. 8). Here Jesus equates this "eternal fire" with the fire of Gehenna. Later, in a prophecy about the coming final judgment, Jesus says that the Son of Man will separate the sheep from the goats. To the sheep he will say, "Come, you who are blessed by my Father, inherit the kingdom prepared for you from the foundation of the world" (25:34). To the goats he will say, "You that are accursed, depart from me into the eternal fire which has been prepared for the devil and his angels" (v. 41). He concludes the prophecy by saying, "These will go away into eternal punishment, but the righteous into eternal life" (v. 46). Jude states that Sodom and Gomorrah, which were destroyed by fire, "are exhibited as an example in undergoing the punishment of eternal fire" (Jude 7 NASB).

The Gospels make other references to fire that we should mention briefly. John the Baptist and Jesus both warn that every tree that fails to produce good fruit will be "cut down and thrown into the fire" (Matt. 3:10; 7:19; Luke 3:9; cf. also John 15:6). In a similar picture, John warns that the Messiah "will gather his wheat into the granary, but the chaff he will burn with unquenchable fire" (Matt. 3:12; Luke 3:17). In Jesus' explanation of his parables, he says that angels will gather the wicked and "will throw them into the furnace of fire, where there will be weeping and gnashing of teeth" (Matt. 13:42, 50).

The Outer Darkness

Jesus associates "weeping and gnashing of teeth" with another description of Hell, that of "the outer darkness." Scandalously, he announces that some Gentiles from far-off lands will be welcomed into the kingdom of heaven while some Jews, "sons of the kingdom," will "be thrown into the outer darkness, where there will be weeping and gnashing of teeth" (Matt. 8:12; similarly Luke 13:28). In his parable of the wedding feast for a king's son, Jesus tells about a man who shows up without wedding attire. The king orders his servants, "Bind him hand and foot, and throw him into the outer darkness, where there will be weeping and gnashing of teeth. For many are called, but few are chosen" (22:13–14). In another parable, Jesus warns that the master of a slave who failed to serve him orders, "As for this worthless slave, throw him into the outer darkness, where there will be weeping and gnashing of teeth" (25:30).

In other places where Jesus does not use the expression "outer darkness," he speaks similarly of the fate of the wicked. Some of those who claim to follow him will ask to be admitted into his presence but will be told, "Go away from me" (Matt. 7:23; Luke 13:27; cf. Matt. 25:41 cited earlier), or will simply be refused entrance (Matt. 25:11–12).

In one of Jesus' parables, the master of an evil slave "will cut him in pieces and put him with the hypocrites, where there will be weeping and gnashing of teeth" (Matt. 24:51). In a parallel passage, Jesus says that the slave's master "will cut him in pieces, and put him with the unfaithful. That slave who knew what his master wanted, but did not prepare himself or do what was wanted, will receive

CHRISTOPHER W. MORGAN

Future punishment is addressed in some way by *every* New Testament author. Matthew, Mark, Luke, John, Paul, James, Peter, Jude, and the unknown author of Hebrews all mention it in their writings. That could not be said of many important truths.[1]

a severe beating. But the one who did not know it and did what deserved a beating will receive a light beating" (Luke 12:46–48).

Fallen angels are also subject to being consigned to darkness; in fact, some are already there: "And the angels who did not keep their own position, but left their proper dwelling, he has kept in eternal chains in deepest darkness for the judgment of the great Day" (Jude 6). As Peter puts it, "God did not spare the angels when they sinned, but cast them into hell and committed them to chains of deepest darkness to be kept until the judgment" (2 Pet. 2:4).

The verb translated "cast into hell" in 2 Peter 2:4 is *tartaroō*, a verb found only here in the Bible. It derives from *Tartaros*, a term for a dark abyss in Greek mythology. Tartarus was said to be as far below Earth — or sometimes, as far below Hades — as the Earth was below the heavens. According to the Greek myth, the Titans (supernatural, demon-like giants) were imprisoned there; the Romans added to the myth and held that wicked people also went to Tartarus. In short, Tartarus was the Greco-Roman equivalent of Hell. Peter does not endorse these myths, but he uses their language about Tartarus to describe the judgment on the fallen angels — and on wicked people as well.

Thus, Peter goes on to say that if God did not spare the angels this punishment and executed other judgments in the past (2 Pet. 2:4–8), then he can "keep the unrighteous under punishment until the day of judgment" (v. 9). The grossly wicked "in their corruption will also be corrupted; they will be wronged as the recompense for their wrongdoing" (vv. 12–13, our translation); "for them the deepest darkness has been reserved" (v. 17).

Eternal Destruction

Jesus and the New Testament writers sometimes describe the final judgment on the wicked using forms of the Greek word *apollymi*, often translated "destruction." We will discuss the meaning of this word in the next chapter, but for now we make note of the key passages (some of which we have discussed previously). Jesus warns that few will find the path to life while many will take the path "that leads to destruction" (Matt. 7:13–14). He tells the disciples to "fear him who can destroy both soul and body in hell" (10:28). The apostle Paul describes the wicked as "vessels of wrath prepared for destruction" (Rom. 9:22 NASB). The apostle Peter compares the Flood, when "the world at that time was destroyed," to a future judgment involving "fire, kept for the day of judgment and destruction of ungodly men" (2 Pet. 3:6–7 NASB).

Paul uses a similar word, *olethron*, in describing the judgment on the wicked: "When they say, 'There is peace and security,' then sudden destruction [*olethron*] will come upon them, as labor pains come upon a pregnant woman, and there will be no escape!" (1 Thess. 5:3). In one of the most important passages on the subject, Paul assures persecuted Christians that God will

> repay with affliction those who afflict you ... when the Lord Jesus is revealed from heaven with his mighty angels in flaming fire, inflicting vengeance on those who do not know God and on those who do not obey the gospel of our Lord Jesus. These will suffer the punishment of eternal destruction [*olethron*], separated from the presence of the Lord and from the glory of his might. (2 Thess. 1:6–9)

A Death Worse than Death

The word *apollymi* and related forms are also frequently used in speaking of a person "losing" his soul, or life, in God's judgment. In one of his most famous paradoxical sayings, which Jesus repeated on several occasions, Jesus warns that those who try to save or keep their lives will "lose" them, whereas those who "lose" their lives for his sake will find them (Matt. 10:39; 16:25–26; Mark 8:35–36; Luke 9:24–25; 17:33). In the Gospel of John, the eternal dimension of the saying is made explicit: "Whoever loves his life loses it, and whoever hates his life in this world will keep it for eternal life" (John 12:25 ESV).

The same word is usually translated "perish" in other contexts pertaining to the judgment on the wicked, as in the most often-quoted verse of the Bible: "For God so loved the world that he gave his only Son, so that everyone who believes in him may not perish but may have eternal life" (John 3:16). Whatever the implications are of perishing, it clearly means loss of life—in this context, loss of eternal life.

The book of Revelation speaks of the future judgment on the wicked as "the second death." It promises that those who overcome by faith "will not be harmed by the second death" (Rev. 2:11). Those who "share in the first resurrection" are blessed because "over these the second death has no power" (20:6). This "second death" is no quiet passing into the night; rather, "this is the second death, the lake of fire" (20:14; see also 21:8).

The Lake of Fire

Some of the most famous and crucial passages about Hell are the passages in the Revelation that speak of "the lake of fire":

> If anyone worships the beast and his image, and receives a mark on his forehead or on his hand, he also will drink of the wine of the wrath of God, which is mixed in full strength in the cup of His anger; and he will be tormented with fire and brimstone in the presence of the holy angels and in the presence of the Lamb. And the smoke of their torment goes up forever and ever; they have no rest day and night. (Rev. 14:9–11 NASB)

> And the beast was captured, and with it the false prophet who performed in its presence the signs by which he deceived those who had received the mark of the beast and those who worshiped its image. These two were thrown alive into the lake of fire that burns with sulfur. (19:20)

> And the devil who had deceived them was thrown into the lake of fire and sulfur, where the beast and the false prophet were; and they will be tormented day and night forever and ever.
> … Then Death and Hades were thrown into the lake of fire. This is the second death, the lake of fire; and anyone whose name was not found written in the book of life was thrown into the lake of fire. (20:10, 14–15)

> But as for the cowardly, the faithless, the polluted, the murderers, the fornicators, the sorcerers, the idolaters, and all liars, their place will be in the lake that burns with fire and sulfur, which is the second death. (21:8)

Although Jesus didn't use the expression "the lake of fire," the idea is consistent with his teaching. The wicked are consigned to it along with the Devil; it is a kind of death; it is pictured as a place of fire; it is a manifestation of God's wrath (see below); and it lasts forever. In all these respects, the book of Revelation is upholding the teaching of Christ.

The Wrath of God

As we have already seen, the New Testament clearly speaks of God's wrath or anger in the context of the final judgment:

- John the Baptist spoke of "the wrath to come" (Matt. 3:7; Luke 3:7).
- Jesus describes the master who throws his unforgiving servant into prison as doing so "in anger" (Matt. 18:34).
- John warns that "he who does not believe the Son shall not see life, but the wrath of God abides on him" (John 3:36 NKJV).
- The unrepentant are storing up for themselves "wrath in the day of wrath and revelation of the righteous judgment of God," who will mete out "indignation and wrath, tribulation and anguish" (Rom. 2:5, 8–9 NKJV).
- Paul describes the wicked as "vessels of wrath" (Rom. 9:22 NASB).
- Before we repented and believed in Christ, we "were by nature children of wrath, like everyone else" (Eph. 2:3).
- It is because of their sins that "the wrath of God is coming on those who are disobedient" (Col. 3:6; Eph. 5:6).
- Paul speaks of Jesus as the one "who rescues us from the wrath that is coming" (1 Thess. 1:10; see also Rom. 5:9; 1 Thess. 5:9).
- In Revelation, the wicked seek in vain to hide "from the face of the one seated on the throne and from the wrath of the Lamb; for the great day of their wrath has come, and who is able to stand?" (Rev. 6:16–17).
- Revelation warns that the wicked "will drink of the wine of God's wrath, poured unmixed into the cup of his anger" (Rev. 14:10).

- Jesus Christ is the agent of God's wrath: "From his mouth comes a sharp sword with which to strike down the nations, and he will rule them with a rod of iron; he will tread the wine press of the fury of the wrath of God the Almighty" (Rev. 19:15).

If all this talk about God's wrath seems intended to scare people, it is. The book of Hebrews says about those who willfully reject the truth about Christ after they learn about it, "there no longer remains a sacrifice for sins, but a fearful prospect of judgment, and a fury of fire that will consume the adversaries" (Heb. 10:26–27). Those who violated the Mosaic covenant died without mercy (v. 28); those who turn their back on the new covenant in Christ will deserve "much worse punishment" (v. 29). "It is a fearful thing to fall into the hands of the living God" (v. 31).

Conclusion: The Myth of the Meek and Mild Jesus

It should be evident from our survey of New Testament teaching about Hell that it is a prominent subject and that Jesus led the way in talking about Hell. Most of the references to this place in the New Testament actually come from Jesus' teaching in the Gospels. He articulated virtually every facet of the doctrine one finds in the rest of the New Testament — the fire, the darkness, the fallen angels, the punishment, the exclusion from God's presence, the loss of life, and the wrath of God.

Nor is there any way to excise Hell from Jesus' teaching by arguing that it represents the views of the Gospel writers or the early church rather than Jesus himself. Hell is a prominent element in the Sermon on the Mount (Matt. 5:21–30; 7:13–14). It is a part of several parables found in different Gospels (e.g., Matt. 18:34–35; Luke 12:46–48). It is expressed in one of Jesus' distinctive sayings, found in all four Gospels, about losing one's life in order to save it (Matt. 16:25–26; Mark 8:35–36; Luke 9:24–25; John 12:25). With the exception of James 3:6, Jesus is the only one to use the term Gehenna anywhere in the New Testament, showing that the term was not a regular part of the early church's vocabulary. In short, impartial tests of authenticity prove that the teaching about Hell in the Gospels does indeed originate from Jesus himself.

Given that Jesus said the kinds of things about Hell recorded in the Gospels, some people today need to revise their view of Jesus. The idea of Jesus as an easy-going fellow who just loved everybody and said only positive, uplifting things is a complete myth. Christian faith, if it is to be faithful to Christ, must acknowledge the reality of Hell.

SENSE

Jesus and the New Testament clearly taught that there will be a Hell.

NONSENSE

Belief in Hell is inconsistent with the spirit of Jesus.

Chapter 11

HELL TO PAY

The wicked check in, but they don't check out.

Perhaps no other element in Christian theology provokes stronger feelings than the subject of Hell. Critics often reach for superlatives in characterizing the doctrine of everlasting conscious punishment as the most vile, cruel idea in the history of humanity. Defenders of the traditional doctrine often argue that denial of Hell as a place of literal fire is a grievous compromise of the Christian faith, impeaching the inspiration of Scripture and undermining the biblical teachings about sin and salvation. Christians who believe in the traditional Hell worry that its denial will keep other Christians from taking the gospel to unbelievers; Christians who don't believe in the traditional Hell worry that its affirmation will keep unbelievers from taking the gospel seriously.

What we propose to do in this chapter and the next is to set out some biblical parameters for a proper view of Hell. (We assume that you have read the previous chapter, where we survey the New Testament's teaching about Hell.) We do not think that we can definitively settle every question on the subject. Our more modest goal is to present a way of thinking about Hell that will avoid certain extremes and shed light on the subject rather than heat—which, if there is any to be shed, belongs in Hell.

Hell's Purpose Is Retribution, Not Restoration

The purpose of Hell is not to make those who go there better people or to help them see the error of their ways and come to repentance. Hell is not like the Betty Ford Clinic. It is not even like a modern prison, where most prisoners are encouraged to become rehabilitated so that they may reenter society as useful citizens. The purpose of Hell is to punish sinners. It is about retribution, not restoration.

The evidence for this thesis in the New Testament is beyond reasonable challenge. God's final disposition toward the wicked is consistently described throughout the New Testament as one of anger and wrath (Matt. 3:7; 18:34; Luke 3:7; John 3:36; Rom. 2:5, 8–9; 5:9; 9:22; Eph. 2:3; 5:6; Col. 3:6; 1 Thess. 1:10; 5:9; Rev. 6:16–17; 14:10; 19:15). Jesus compares Hell to a prison where offenders are tortured for their crimes (Matt. 5:25–26; 18:34–35; Luke 12:47–48, 58–59). Those in Hell will receive "eternal punishment [*kolasis*]" (Matt. 25:46). Some critics of the doctrine of Hell engage in word games with the Greek word *kolasis*,[1] but there is no question that it means punishment, since in context it means being cast into the eternal fire prepared for the Devil and his angels (Matt. 25:41). Peter said that "the unrighteous," like wicked angels, are being kept "under punishment" while awaiting the final judgment (2 Pet. 2:9).

The other major Greek word for punishment, *timōria*, appears in the statement in Hebrews that those who renounce faith in Christ deserve "much worse punishment" than those who repudiated the Mosaic covenant (Heb. 10:28–29).

PAUL HELM

One important reason for a Christian accepting that hell is a place of justice is because Christ, whose moral understanding was not warped or twisted as ours is, and who fully represented the moral character of God, saw no injustice in hell.[2]

Moreover, Paul writes to Christians in Thessalonica that Christ will "repay with affliction those who afflict you," and that when he comes, he will be "inflicting vengeance [*ekdikēsis*]" (2 Thess. 1:6–9). *Ekdikēsis* can also be translated "revenge" or "retribution"; Jesus is going to make them pay! That may sound shocking to some people today, but not to those who have suffered greatly for their faith in Christ.

In contrast to these numerous and explicit statements about the purpose of Hell, one searches in vain for any clear indication that anyone will ever emerge from Hell, let alone emerge reformed or restored. Some might suppose that Jesus' comparisons of the wicked being punished in Hell to prisoners suffering until they "pay" their debt (Matt. 5:25–26; 18:34–35; Luke 12:58–59) might offer such hope. Not so. In Jesus' parable of the unforgiving servant, his debt to the master (representing God) is said to be ten thousand talents, whereas his fellow servant's debt to him was a hundred denarii (Matt. 18:24, 28). To put these numbers in perspective, one denarius was the typical wage paid to a servant in Jesus' day, so that a debt of a hundred denarii was a considerable sum (equivalent to several thousand dollars today). However, a talent was equivalent to six or ten thousand denarii (probably the latter in this context). For a servant to earn just *one* talent would require, then, more than twenty-five years. Ten thousand talents was a ridiculously huge debt—one that would take such a servant more than a quarter of a million years to discharge. It would be comparable to someone working a minimum wage job owing his company something like five *billion* dollars. The point of the story is that it's hopeless—the debt can never be paid and the debtor will never get out of prison.

Jesus' parable directly challenges the common sentiment that sending someone to Hell for eternity is out of proportion, that the punishment does not fit the crime. He characterizes the "debt" that we owe to God as an astronomical sum. The servant's debt to his master is *a million times greater* than the substantial debt his fellow servant owed to him. That is the way Jesus pictures for us the enormity of our sin in God's eyes.

Hell's Punishment Is Just, Not Vindictive

Lest Jesus' teaching on Hell be misunderstood, it is essential to the doctrine that whatever punishment is meted out in Hell will be just. Critics sometimes caricature Christianity as teaching that a kindly old nonreligious grandmother will get the same punishment as Adolf Hitler. This is simply not the case. God is not sadistic or in any way unjust. His anger or wrath is a righteous anger. Whatever Hell will be like and whoever ends up there, it will not be unfair, unjust, or out of proportion. Abraham recognized that it would not be in character for God to treat "the righteous and the wicked" alike and asked, "Shall not the Judge of all the earth do what is just?" (Gen. 18:25). This principle of justice is basic to the biblical doctrine of Hell.

That is why Jesus taught that there will be varying degrees of punishment in Hell. "That slave who knew what his master wanted, but did not prepare himself or do what was wanted, will receive a severe beating. But the one who did not know and did what deserved a beating will receive a light beating" (Luke 12:47–48). Ignorance of God's will does not entirely exonerate a sinner, since to some extent all human beings have a knowledge of God's standards of right and wrong (Rom. 2:14–16), but it is treated as a significant mitigating factor. Hell will not be one-size-fits-all.

Non-Christians may be interested to know that the punishment of Hell will be especially severe on professing Christians who belie their profession by their actions. Jesus' parable of the slave who knew his master's will but ignored it getting many lashes makes this point. So does Peter's warning that for those who knew Christ but then returned to worldly living, "the last state has become worse for them than the first. For it would have been better for them never to have known the way of righteousness than, after knowing it, to turn back from the holy commandment that was passed on to them" (2 Pet. 2:20–21). Similarly,

> Hell will not be one-size-fits-all.

Hebrews warns that those who abandon faith in Christ will deserve "much worse punishment" than did Jews who violated the Mosaic covenant (Heb. 10:28–29).

Hell's Period Is Permanent, Not Temporary

The conclusion that Hell will be permanent follows from the point made earlier that its purpose is to punish sinners for a debt that can never be repaid. But we are not dependent on inference for this understanding.

(1) The New Testament explicitly teaches that the Devil and other wicked angels will be sent to Hell forever. Jesus described Hell as a place of "eternal fire" for the Devil and his angels (Matt. 25:41). Some wicked angels are already "kept in eternal bonds" (Jude 6 NASB). It has been said that these "bonds" will not actually be "eternal" because the "imprisonment is only temporary, until the Day of Judgment when they will be transferred to the fire of Gehenna."[3] But surely we are not to understand that these wicked angels will be *released* from their bonds; rather, they will never be free but will simply be "transferred" (an appropriate term here) to their final imprisonment in Hell. Either way, the sentence of Hell is clearly eternal. The devil (along with the beast and the false prophet) will be cast into the lake of fire, where "they will be tormented day and night forever and ever" (Rev. 20:10).

(2) Human beings will also be consigned to Hell forever. Jesus warns that anything is better than being cast into "the eternal fire" of Gehenna (Matt. 18:8–9). The wicked will depart and go away into "eternal punishment" along with the Devil and his angels (Matt. 25:41, 46). Paul affirms that the wicked will suffer "the punishment of eternal destruction" (2 Thess. 1:9). Those who align themselves with the beast "will be tormented with fire and sulfur.... And the smoke of their torment goes up forever and ever. There is no rest day and night" (Rev. 14:9–11).

We have already explained (in ch. 9) why "eternal" is a correct translation in passages such as Matthew 25:46. The New Testament uses other words and phrases, such as "forever and ever," to express the same idea. It is simply not plausible to view Hell as a temporary condition. Whatever it is, Hell is a one-way trip.

Hell's State Is Death, Not Life

In popular explanations of Hell, one often hears that people will live forever either in Heaven or Hell. This way of speaking of Hell is, we will argue, getting at something that is true but is not worded in the best way. Biblically speaking, the righteous will live forever in Heaven (or rather the New Heavens and New Earth), but the wicked will not "live" forever in Hell.

Jesus, for example, says that the righteous will enjoy "eternal life" but the wicked will be consigned to "eternal punishment" (Matt. 25:41; cf. Dan. 12:2). These are evidently mutually exclusive options; the wicked will *not* have eternal life. The righteous will have a "resurrection of life" while the wicked face a "resurrection of condemnation" (John 5:29). Whereas physical death kills only the body, Hell is the death of both body and soul (Matt. 10:28).

The rest of the New Testament reflects this same perspective. As Paul famously puts it, "the wages of sin is death, but the free gift of God is eternal life in Christ Jesus our Lord" (Rom. 6:23). Perhaps most explicitly, the book of Revelation refers to the final disposition of the wicked as "the second death" (Rev. 2:11; 20:6, 14; 21:8). This expression matches perfectly Jesus' teaching about Hell as the death not only of the body but also of the soul. Whereas believers are born again (John 3:3, 5) and thus have the promise of eternal life, unbelievers face the prospect of a second death and eternal condemnation.

Hell's Result Is Endless Death, Not Ended Existence

Those who view death as the cessation of a person's existence (such as Jehovah's Witnesses) naturally and consistently view Hell as a final passing into nonexistence. (Indeed, this is the reason *why* they define dying as ceasing to exist—in order to understand Hell in the same way.) However, we have already seen that the Bible does not sustain the idea of death as becoming nonexistent. Human beings continue to exist even after their physical deaths, albeit in an incomplete state (see chs. 4–6). As we said in chapter 5, the state of the lost in Hell may be described as *anti-life*.

For persons, life means light, wholeness (the Hebrew *shalom*, "peace"), and relationship with God (John 1:4; 17:3; Rom. 8:6). Death is the last great enemy, the power that Christ came to break for those who believe in him (1 Cor. 15:26, 54–57). For the unredeemed, death will be God's final judgment. In "the second death" they will not be merely incomplete, but utterly devoid of life; they will be in complete darkness, shattered beyond repair, separated forever from the presence of God, and cut off from his benevolence, his providential care, and his grace.

Admittedly, an existence in darkness and hopeless separation from God, love, light, and life isn't much of an existence. Various Christian thinkers, especially in the past century, have explored ways of understanding Hell as a kind of negation, a sort of cosmic void, lacking existence in a full-bodied, robust sense.

Perhaps the most famous advocate of such a view was C. S. Lewis. In *The Problem of Pain*, Lewis argued that the occupants in Hell are far less than human: "To enter Heaven is to become more human than you ever succeeded in being in earth; to enter Hell, is to be banished from humanity. What is cast (or casts itself) into Hell is not a man: it is 'remains.'"[4] Although Lewis's explanations go beyond what we can clearly demonstrate from Scripture, they suggest a way of thinking that is faithful to it. Our view of Hell must take fully into account that it is sheer death and that it means torment without rest forever. There is room for creative proposals and for disagreements about just what Hell will be like as long as we stay within the parameters of the full teaching of the Bible on the subject.

Those who view death as annihilation or nonexistence regard the biblical motif of Hell as destruction as primary in thinking about the nature of Hell. The main words for "destroy" and "destruction" in biblical Greek are forms of *apollymi*. It will not do to pit other motifs associated with Hell, such as separation and torment, against the motif of destruction; all of these ways of describing Hell are biblical and all must be taken into consideration.

In the Greek Old Testament, *apollymi* has a range of uses. It is used of the destruction of Sodom and Gomorrah, which meant the obliteration of the cities and of their inhabitants (Gen. 18:24, 28–32; 19:13; cf. Luke 17:29). Annihilationists regard this usage, and this passage, as a paradigm or model of the "destruction" brought by God's judgment. However, other passages about divine judgment exhibit a different usage. The plagues resulted in Egypt being "ruined" (Ex. 10:7 NIV, NRSV, NLT). Clearly, Egypt did not cease to exist. Disobedience to certain laws was to be punished by the offender being "cut off" (Heb.) from the people (Ex. 30:38; Lev. 7:20–21, 25, 27; 17:10; 20:3, 5–6; 23:30). God threatens the nation of Israel that he will "dispossess" them for their rebellion (Num. 14:12; cf. Deut. 4:26). The rebels led by Korah "went down alive into Sheol ... and they *perished* from the midst of the assembly" (Num. 16:33; cf. Jude 11).

Several New Testament passages using a form of *apollymi* do so in reference to ruin, waste, loss, or perishing[5]:

- Wineskins can be "ruined" (Matt. 9:17; Mark 2:22; Luke 5:37).[6]
- A sheep (Luke 15:2, 4; cf. Ps. 119:176), a coin (Luke 15:8–9), and even a son (Luke 15:24, 32) can be "lost."
- Israel can be described as "lost" sheep (Matt. 10:6; 15:24).
- A person can either "lose" his soul, or he can find or keep his soul (Matt. 10:39; 16:25; Mark 8:35; Luke 9:24–25; 17:33; John 12:25).
- A reward can be "lost" (Matt. 10:42; Mark 9:41).
- Food can "perish" (John 6:27).
- Perfume can be "wasted" (Matt. 26:8; Mark 14:4).
- A flower's beauty can be "lost" (James 1:11 NET).
- Gold pieces can "perish" in fire (1 Pet. 1:7).
- Luxuries can be "lost" (Rev. 18:14).

A judicious interpretation of biblical passages that speak of Hell using forms of *apollymi* must consider the range of meanings that the word has while allowing context to be the dominant factor in deciding what nuance applies in those passages. As we suggested in chapter 5, destruction is a relative concept and can connote anything from waste and ruin to obliteration and annihilation. In Hell a person loses life forever (Matt. 10:39, etc.) and is ruined (Rom. 9:22; 1 Cor. 3:17), and his life is destroyed (2 Pet. 3:7, 9). There is nothing good left, and what is left is not much.

SENSE

The wicked will be punished forever in Hell.

NONSENSE

Hell is a reformatory for wayward souls.

Chapter 12

THE ETERNAL FIRE

The fire of Hell represents a terrifying reality to be avoided at all cost.

So far we have seen that those who go to Hell stay there forever, never to be released. They go there to be punished for their sins, not to be rehabilitated for life in Heaven. They will still exist, but not as whole persons; their existence will be an endless death, not eternal life.

But what about the fire? Will the wicked literally burn in Hell? If not, what does the fire represent? We will conclude our discussion of Hell with a consideration of these questions.

Hell's Condition Is Painful, Not Pain-Free

We have touched on the fact repeatedly that Hell will be painful. The New Testament describes it as a place of fiery torment, of punishment, of affliction, of weeping and gnashing of teeth. It is understandable that many people want to find a way around such language, but efforts to do so fall short.

Edward Fudge regards the judgment on Sodom and Gomorrah as a type of Hell (rightly so), and he points out that the cities were completely destroyed. Citing the description of smoke rising from the plain as from a furnace (Gen. 19:28), he declares, "Throughout Scripture from this point, rising smoke symbolizes complete destruction (Is 34:10; Rev 14:11; 19:3)."[1] According to Fudge,

Jude 7 "calls the fire that fell from heaven and destroyed Sodom 'eternal fire,'" meaning, "It is a fire that destroys sinners totally and forever." Therefore, when the Bible speaks of Hell as "eternal fire," it means only that those who go to Hell will be completely eliminated from existence forever.[2]

Jude 7 does not exactly say that Sodom was destroyed by "eternal fire." What it says is that Sodom and the other wicked cities around them serve as an example in undergoing the punishment of eternal fire.[3] The point Jude is making is that the fire that fell on those cities typifies the punishment that will come on the false teachers who are trying to mislead Jude's readers. He calls the fire that fell on those cities "eternal fire" because it foreshadows a future "fire" that really will be eternal.

Although Jude 7 might, depending on how one reads it, be viewed as proof that the term "eternal fire" *could* be used of a fire that simply annihilates, it does not prove that this or similar expressions *always* have that meaning. We must look at each occurrence in context. The "eternal fire" of which Jesus speaks in Matthew 25:41 is described as a fire "prepared for the devil and his angels," suggesting that it is a very different sort of phenomenon. When Jesus in this context says that the "goats" will be told, "Depart from me," and that they "will go away into eternal punishment" (vv. 41, 46), it makes sense to infer that the fire will really be eternal, just as the punishment will be. Even Fudge agrees that the punishment will be eternal, while being careful to deny that this will mean eternal *punishing*. But if, as Fudge admits, the punishment will be eternal, then so will the fire.

Another problem with Fudge's argument is with his list of biblical references for the idea that "rising smoke symbolizes complete destruction." At least one of the three texts he cites is talking about Hell (Rev. 14:11),[4] and the Old Testament text is talking about a judgment that is a type of Hell (Isa. 34:10; see vv. 2–9). Revelation does not say merely that the smoke rises forever. Perhaps that statement alone would not prove that the wicked exist forever in Hell. But it says more—that the wicked people "will be tormented," that they will have "no rest day and night," and even that the Devil, the beast, and the false prophet "will be tormented day and night forever and ever" (Rev. 14:9–11; cf. 20:10). The description of what will happen to the wicked angels and humans goes beyond Old Testament types and indicates explicitly that these wicked beings will suffer forever.

A plausible response to the evidence from Revelation is to argue that the language should not be taken literally because the book uses obvious symbolic imagery, typical of ancient Jewish "apocalyptic" literature. One may agree not to take the language literally (as we will argue below), but it must mean something. Furthermore, it is not only the book of Revelation, or apocalyptic literature, that describes the wicked suffering in Hell. Jesus speaks of the wicked being tortured or punished in Hell; he says that they will weep and gnash their teeth in Hell and that some will receive a greater amount of punishment than others.

Not all of these statements come in Jesus' parables (though several do); for example, when Jesus speaks about the wicked being cast into the fiery furnace and weeping and gnashing their teeth there, those comments come in Jesus' *explanation* of one of his parables (Matt. 13:40–42). Similarly, when Paul talks about those who afflicted believers being afflicted in the final judgment (2 Thess. 1:6), he is saying this in one of his epistles, in a context that seems lacking in figurative language or apocalyptic imagery (2 Thess. 1:3–12). It is difficult to see how all these references to torture, torment, affliction, beatings, punishment, and similar language can all be neatly explained to mean quiet passing into nonexistence.

> Jesus did not say that the wicked will weep and gnash their teeth at the prospect of Hell or on their way into Hell. He said they would weep and gnash their teeth *in Hell*.

Indeed, Fudge agrees. He states in several places that the wicked will suffer for some unspecified period of time, to an extent determined by God's justice, and then be annihilated. Regarding the weeping and gnashing of teeth, he comments: "These verbs do speak of conscious suffering which precedes final destruction; the wicked do not happily and quietly fade away."[5] With regard to the suffering of the wicked in Revelation 14:9–11, Fudge writes, "Guillebaud is therefore correct when he writes that these words ['day or night' in Rev. 14:11] 'certainly say that there will be no break or intermission in the suffering of the followers of the Beast, *while it continues*; but in themselves they do not say that it will continue for ever.'"[6] So Fudge understands at least some of the New Testament descriptions of the wicked suffering to mean that they will indeed suffer. The only disagreement (albeit a significant one) is whether this suffering will be in some sense everlasting or eternal.

The problem is that in admitting any suffering associated with Hell, Fudge has opened the door to eternal punishment in Hell. Jesus did not say that the wicked will weep and gnash their teeth at the prospect of Hell or on their way into Hell. He said they would weep and gnash their teeth *in Hell* (in "the furnace of fire" or "the outer darkness," Matt. 8:12; 13:42; 22:13–14; 24:51; 25:30; Luke 13:28). John says that the beast, the false prophet, and the Devil will be tormented *in* the lake of fire (Rev. 20:10), after having been cast into it—and that this torment will go on forever.

In this regard, Guillebaud, whom Fudge cites, is right. Saying that those suffering have no rest "day or night" does not prove eternal suffering because those words "in themselves they do not say that it will continue for ever." But even when the words "day and night" are directly put together with "forever and ever," as they are in Revelation 20:10, annihilationists refuse to acknowledge that the torment continues forever—or even that anything will exist to be "tormented" (whether literally *or* figuratively).

One common argument against understanding Revelation 20:10 to be referring to unending torment is that the beast and the false prophet are either "institutions" or "personified forces of evil," not persons, and if they "are not persons," then they cannot actually be tormented.[7] Then what does the text mean when it says they are tortured? No explanation is given. Fudge, for example, makes no attempt to explain what the torture might represent, contenting himself with assuring his readers that the lake of fire represents annihilation.

The argument's assumption that the beast and the false prophet do not represent persons is also open to challenge. Assuming for the sake of argument that they do represent institutions, those institutions would be comprised of *persons* acting in cooperation. In that case, the casting of the beast and the false prophet into the lake of fire would refer to the consignment of the people running those institutions to eternal punishment. If we prefer to think of the beast and the false prophet as personifications of evil, those evils are still "incarnated" in real people who "embody" the anti-God values of the beast, and so again the passage might in fact be referring to the punishment of actual people.

Of course, the Devil *is* (as Fudge and others admit) a person. So, will he be tortured in Hell? Fudge draws a blank on this aspect of the passage; all he says about it is, "There is no easy solution." He then quickly changes the subject and points out, "Yet to this point no human beings are involved in the lake of fire, nor does this passage say that any of Adam's race are tormented for ever and ever."[8] Similarly, David Powys argues that "ongoing torture in the 'lake of fire' is not attributed to any humans (unless the beast and the false prophet are human).... In terms of the present study the critical finding is that if the lake of fire will constitute literal torment for any, it will be so only for the beast, the false prophet and Satan."[9]

This objection is essentially an argument from silence and very much misses the point (while inviting the question whether it is morally acceptable for God to consign the Devil to eternal torment but not humans). By saying that wicked human beings will be consigned to the lake of fire along with the Devil and his allies, John is simply affirming Jesus' teaching that wicked humans will

G. K. BEALE

That this is a real, ongoing suffering for those represented by the images of "beast and false prophet" is apparent, since the same expression of eternal punishment applies to the *individual* devil in this verse [Rev. 20:10] and since virtually the same expression is applied to the *individual* followers of the beast in 14:10–11.[10]

be consigned to the same fate already intended for the Devil and his angels (Matt. 25:41).

The point of these statements is to warn people that if they follow the Devil, they will share his fate. It makes no sense to try to insinuate into these passages the notion that human beings might go to the same eternal fire, the same lake of fire, where the Devil will be tormented day and night forever and ever, but somehow (despite the explicit statement in Rev. 14:9–11 that those who follow the beast will be tormented) those human beings might not suffer the same kind of fate. While their suffering will no doubt be less severe than that of the Devil (cf. Luke 12:46–48), evidently they *will* suffer.

It is our assessment that nothing the Bible says or could say will convince a committed annihilationist. The Bible's references to eternal fire, eternal punishment, and even torment day and night forever and ever do not convince them. What could the Bible be able to say that would prove endless torment to them? The Bible doesn't use the expression "endless torment" (though surely "torment ... forever and ever" is the equivalent); even if it did, annihilationists would try to explain it away in the same way they do the language actually found in the Bible.

Hell's Suffering Is Spiritual, Not Physical

We contend that the suffering or pain of those consigned to Hell will be a spiritual form of suffering, not physical pain. The evidence for this conclusion is disarmingly simple. Jesus says that wicked people will be sent away "into the eternal fire prepared for the devil and his angels" (Matt. 25:41). Since the Devil and his angels are spiritual beings, not physical beings, Jesus' statement can only mean that the "eternal fire" is a form of punishment designed for spiritual beings. The implication is that the suffering of the condemned human beings in Hell will also be a spiritual type of suffering. It will consist of spiritual or mental anguish, perhaps in the form of regret, an abiding sense of loss, and the devastation of permanent exile from God, the world, and all that is good, beautiful, whole, and meaningful.

Only if the "fire" of Hell is interpreted to mean literal, physical fire can the suffering of Hell be understood to mean physical pain. But how could nonphysical entities, such as the Devil and his angels, be in any way affected by physical fire? But if we deny that the fire is physical, are we not denying the reality of Hell? This leads us to our last thesis.

Hell's Fire Is Symbolic, Not Literal

Unfortunately, people on both sides of the argument over Hell have confused the issue by equating a denial that the fire of Hell is *literal* with a denial that the suffering of Hell symbolized by the fire is *real*. Hell will be real enough; its "fire" will be devastating, painful, and terrible. To say that the fire will not be "literal" does not mean that Hell will be a calm nothingness.

The fact is that some of the most conservative Christian theologians have long recognized the figurative nature of the biblical descriptions of Hell without compromising their terror (see following quotes). Augustine, while preferring the view that the fire of Hell would afflict the body, recognized that others even in his day viewed the fire as descriptive of the spiritual suffering of those in Hell.[11] We think this view has the better argument biblically.

A variety of recognized students of the Bible over the centuries have understood the fires of Hell as figurative.

The devil and his demons and the man that is his, that is the Antichrist and the impious and the sinful, will be given over to everlasting fire: not material fire like our fire, but such fire as God would know. (John of Damascus, eighth century)[12]

Now, because no description can deal adequately with the gravity of God's vengeance against the wicked, their torments and tortures are figuratively expressed to us by physical things, that is, by darkness, weeping, and gnashing of teeth [Matt. 8:12; 22:13], unquenchable fire [Matt. 3:12; Mark 9:43; Isa. 66:24], an undying worm gnawing at the heart [Isa. 66:24]. (John Calvin, sixteenth century)[13]

Sensible figures are employed to describe the misery of hell, as they are to describe the blessedness of heaven. It cannot be inferred from the mere use of metaphors that the duration of either is temporary. (William Shedd, nineteenth century)[14]

Fire in Scripture is a symbol of the painful torments of hell.... Even if the language [for Heaven and Hell] is highly figurative, the figures convey two radically different situations of conscious joy and conscious torment after death. (Gordon Lewis and Bruce Demarest, twentieth century)[15]

The "lake of fire" in Rev. 20:10 is not literal since Satan (along with his angels) is a spiritual being. The "fire" is a punishment that is not physical but spiritual in nature. (Greg Beale, twentieth century)[16]

The problem of a literal approach to the biblical descriptions of Hell as fire may be illustrated from a popular physical explanation of Hell. J. Dwight Pentecost, in his influential book *Things to Come*, followed a certain C. T. Schwartze in speculating that the lake of fire might be literally just that. Pentecost quotes Schwartze's article:

The word lake must connote a body of matter having liquid form. Therefore, if Scripture is truth, this eternal fire must be in liquid form ... the very simple proof of the portions of Scripture we have been discussing *lies in the existence of the singular phenomena of the skies known as the midget or white dwarf stars!* ... The white dwarf, to all intents, *can never burn out*.... Although we cannot say that God will actually use these lakes of fire in fulfilling His Word, the answer to the skeptic is in the heavens where there *are* lakes of fire.[17]

The white-dwarf theory runs into a bit of scientific trouble, since a white dwarf cannot be described as liquid in form. White dwarf stars are the remnants of stars that have burned out and shed most of their material; all that remains is a hot core that is extremely compacted and dense and therefore not liquid.

The theory that the lake of fire will be a star was endorsed tentatively by Henry Morris, best known as an advocate of young-earth creationism: "A star, after all, is precisely that, a lake of fire." Morris, however, suggested that the lake of fire might turn out to be "a 'black hole,' if and when such objects are actually proven to exist."[18] Morris's book was published in 1983, before the evidence for black holes was as plentiful as it is now. Unfortunately, even in 1983 it was known that a black hole does not have any fire. In fact, the conventional view was and still is that a black hole forms when a huge star that has completely burned itself out collapses in on itself. Neither the white-dwarf theory nor the black-hole theory can explain the presence of sulfur ("brimstone") in the lake of fire, if it is to be taken literally (Rev. 14:10; 19:20; 20:10; 21:8). Sulfur is a relatively heavy element that would not be present in any sort of dead or collapsed star, white dwarf, or black hole.

John Walvoord, in his contribution to the book *Four Views on Hell*, briefly defends the view that the fire of Hell will be literal fire. According to Walvoord, "Scripture never challenges the concept that eternal punishment is by literal fire."[19] Actually, as several theologians have observed, the Bible depicts Hell using a variety of images or themes that, if combined, cannot be taken literally. The Bible's imagery for Hell sometimes is inconsistent with the fire being literal, as when Hell is described as a place of darkness (e.g., Matt. 8:12; 22:13; 25:30; 2 Pet. 2:17; Jude 6, 13). Literal fire is also incompatible with the imagery of the body being eaten by worms (Isa. 66:24; Mark 9:48). Of course, literal fire is inconsistent with the person continuing to exist forever in torment, since literal, physical fire would soon reduce the person's physical body to ashes (and would do nothing to the person's immaterial soul or spirit).

> Setting aside all other possible objections, we are compelled to ask how a white dwarf star, a black hole, or any other physical phenomenon could hold, let alone torment, the Devil and his angels.

We are not saying that the biblical language about Hell is inconsistent. There is in fact no problem reconciling the various biblical descriptions of Hell—*if* we recognize them as symbolic pictures of a hellish reality.

In his response to William Crockett's "Metaphorical View," Walvoord charges that interpreting the fire of Hell metaphorically impugns the "inerrancy" and "accuracy" of Scripture. He complains that those who interpret Hell in a nonliteral way "do not want to accept what the Bible teaches" and that their main argument against literal fire in Hell is that the idea is "repulsive."[20] These criticisms are as false as they are common. It is precisely because we want to accept all of what the Bible teaches about Hell that we embrace the view that there will be endless torment in Hell, but it will be spiritual rather than physical in nature.

Walvoord's accusations also draw the battle lines on this subject in the wrong place. Those who think of Hell fire as physical fire and those who think of it as a metaphor for spiritual torment both agree that the wicked will exist in Hell and will be punished there forever. That is a hard enough truth for many people in our society to accept.

SENSE

The biblical descriptions of Hell cannot be taken literally.

NONSENSE

If Hell is not literal, then it won't be painful.

Chapter 13

ONE WAY, ONE TRUTH

Jesus is the only Savior from Hell and the only Way to Heaven.

As troubling as some people find the idea of Hell, what really bothers people is the thought of who might go there. We mentioned at the beginning of chapter 9 that about two-fifths of American non-Christians acknowledge the existence of Hell, though most don't expect to go there. Presumably they are comfortable with the idea of oppressive dictators, mass murderers, and terrorists going to Hell. What really offends many people—let's be honest—is the idea that non-Christians in general are going to Hell. Ranking toward the top of the list of objections to a biblical, evangelical Christian faith is the complaint that it unfairly consigns most of humanity, including those who have never heard of Christ, to Hell.

There are actually two distinct questions here. The first is whether Jesus Christ is the only way of salvation. The second question is whether anyone can be saved who has not heard the gospel message about Jesus Christ and consciously believed in him in this life. We will address the first question in this chapter and the second question in the following two chapters.

First Things First

We will not be able to think clearly about this subject unless we already have certain other more foundational questions answered.

We must first have it settled in our minds that *Christianity is true*—that God exists, that he created the world, that we are subject to his rule, that the human race has fallen into sin, corruption, and death, and that Jesus Christ died on the cross and rose from the dead to redeem sinners. For anyone not yet convinced that Christ is the proper object of faith, the question of whether anyone can be saved apart from faith in Christ is moot. If you haven't settled the issue of whether you should put your faith in Christ, we would suggest that you make that issue your top priority.[1]

Of course, as we have already acknowledged, some non-Christians cite the problem of the fate of those who haven't heard the gospel as a reason to question the gospel. This may sound cold, but such an objection is completely irrelevant. Does the question of what happens to the unevangelized have any bearing on whether there is good evidence for God's existence? Suppose the Bible gives an answer to the question of the unevangelized that we don't like. Would that somehow prove that Jesus didn't rise from the dead? Not at all.

We are not suggesting that there is something wrong with non-Christians asking this or any other question. Fire away, we say! But we are trying to explain that the truth of our answer presupposes that certain other, more fundamental questions have already been answered. We would be among the first to say that if Jesus didn't rise from the dead, there would be no point at all in worrying about whether everyone has heard the gospel, because the gospel would be false. But if Jesus did rise from the dead, the gospel is true, although of course some Christians' understanding of the gospel might not be completely accurate.

Indeed, what some Christians think about the fate of the unevangelized is bound to be inaccurate, since there is a diversity of views on the subject among Christians. That's another reason not to prejudge the truth of Christianity on the basis of an answer to the question of what happens to those who haven't heard.

Moreover, we must agree that *the Bible is authoritative in what it teaches* on the matter of what will happen to those who have not heard the gospel. After all, if the Bible is not trustworthy on this subject, no other source is, and there would be no way to answer the question with any reliability. Again, we encourage those who are unconvinced of the reliability and inspiration of the Bible to investigate that question.

Finally, we must agree that *at least some people will not be saved*. We have explained our reasons for this conclusion in the preceding four chapters. If no one is going to Hell, then obviously people who haven't heard the gospel won't be going there. If everyone is going to be saved, then again, those who haven't heard are certain to be among those who will be saved. Regrettably, not everyone will be saved, as we have explained (see especially ch. 9). This still leaves wide open the question of who will be saved and who will not.

In the rest of this chapter, we will attempt to provide a biblical framework for thinking about this subject. We admit that we don't know with certainty the answers to all of the questions people ask on this subject. But we do think it is possible to have a clear enough understanding of the subject to meet our legitimate need to know.

Some Who Claim to Be Christians Will Be Lost

Perhaps a good place to begin is with the observation that not everyone who claims to be a Christian will be saved. We have this on pretty good authority—that of Jesus Christ himself:

> Not everyone who says to me, "Lord, Lord," will enter the kingdom of heaven, but only the one who does the will of my Father in heaven. On that day many will say to me, "Lord, Lord, did we not prophesy in your name, and cast out demons in your name, and do many deeds of power in your name?" Then I will declare to them, "I never knew you; go away from me, you evildoers." (Matt. 7:21–23)

The biblical position simply cannot be reduced to the claim that "everyone in our religion is saved and everyone else is lost." (Substitute "denomination," "association," or any equivalent term for "religion" and the point still holds.) We are not espousing the notion that membership in our religion, or our church, comes with a free pass to Heaven. In fact, as we pointed out earlier, we fully expect that some of the members of our churches are going to get an especially severe punishment in Hell! The reason for this is that *God will judge people based on what they know.*

James warns his readers to be cautious about becoming teachers, "for you know that we who teach will be judged with greater strictness" (James 3:1). In one of Jesus' parables (Luke 12:42–48), the servant who knew his master's will but didn't do it received a heavy punishment, while the servant who didn't know, although still doing things worthy of punishment, got a relatively light sentence. The principle that Jesus enunciates at the end of this parable is clear: "From everyone to whom much has been given, much will be required" (Luke 12:48).

Jesus Is the Only Source of Salvation

The New Testament is crystal clear in teaching that whoever will be saved, in any period of human history, will have been saved by the redemptive suffering, death, and resurrection of Jesus Christ. Two key statements in this regard, one from Jesus himself and one from the apostle Peter, are as explicit as they are famous:

> I am the way, and the truth, and the life. No one comes to the Father except through me. (John 14:6)

> And there is salvation in no one else, for there is no other name under heaven that has been given among people by which we must be saved. (Acts 4:12)

Why is it that people can only be saved if they are saved by Jesus? (1) First of all, *they cannot save themselves.* People cannot make themselves good enough for God or make themselves right with God, based on what they do. This is the explicit teaching of Paul: "For 'no human being will be justified in his sight' by deeds prescribed by the law, for through the law comes the knowledge of sin" (Rom. 3:20). In other words, the Law of Moses does not give us a way to be justified, or considered right, in God's sight; instead, it simply tells us what sin is and shows that we are sinners.[2]

If a person could get right with God by doing enough good works, then there might be some hope for people to gain eternal life without Christ's help. Unfortunately, none of us can pull it off, "for all have sinned and fall short of the glory of God, and they are now justified by his grace as a gift, through the redemption that is in Christ Jesus" (Rom. 3:23–24 ESV). This doesn't mean that Christians don't do good works—if they don't, their claim to believe is questionable—but that their relationship with God is not the result of their works but rather the result of God's gracious acceptance of them because of what Jesus did:

> For by grace you have been saved through faith, and this is not your own doing; it is the gift of God—not the result of works, so that no one may boast. For we are what he has made us, created in Christ Jesus for good works, which God prepared beforehand to be our way of life. (Eph. 2:8–10)

If Christians cannot and do not save themselves by their works, it follows that no one else does either. Paul says explicitly that "no flesh" will be saved in that way.

(2) *God has chosen to save people throughout the world through his Son, Jesus Christ.* Those passages misunderstood by universalists as teaching that everyone will be saved come into play here (see chapter 9). "For God so loved the world that he gave his only Son, so that everyone who believes in him may not perish but may have eternal life" (John 3:16). Jesus is the Savior for the world, dying to atone for the sins of people throughout the world, bringing reconciliation to the world and justification to all people (John 1:29; 4:42; 1 John 2:2; 4:14; Rom. 5:18; 2 Cor. 5:19; Col. 1:19–20; 1 Tim. 2:6). We can speculate all day long as to whether God might have chosen to save people in another way, but the fact is that we have no reliable way of knowing, and in fact Scripture says he has chosen this one way and no other.

We say this with all sincere respect for the teachings of other religions. Judaism, from which Christianity emerged, includes in

C. S. LEWIS

The people who keep on asking if they can't lead a decent life without Christ, don't know what life is about.[3]

its heritage God's revelation in the Old Testament. Islam borrowed generously from both Judaism and Christianity, affirms one Creator God, and promotes a system of values that while different from Christianity at key points is also in many respects noble and biblically rooted. Buddhism is admirable in recognizing the pervasiveness of suffering in the human condition and in its aspirations for peace and contentment.

It is not necessary or desirable from our perspective as Christians to denigrate what is good and true in other religions. We simply point out that none of them offers a way of forgiveness revealed and authorized by God to those alienated from God by their sins. Buddhism in most of its forms does not even recognize the existence of a personal Creator God to whom we are accountable. Islam does, thankfully, but it teaches that people must prove themselves worthy by submission to what Muslims believe is the will of God. Sadly, Islam as a religion rejects the biblical teaching that Jesus died for our sins and rose from the dead. Judaism, though its roots are in the Old Testament, is no longer the religion of the Old Testament; it has no sacrifices for sins. Tragically, Judaism does not acknowledge the Messiah whom God sent to the Jews.

The Christian claim that Jesus is the only Savior is not a parochial, narrow-minded position. It is the truth. Among the world's major religions, Jesus is truly the only Savior on the market.[4] This fact may or may not imply that adherents of non-Christian religions are necessarily lost, but it clearly means that none of those religions are paths to salvation. In other words, if adherents of other religions end up being saved, it will not be because they followed their religion. God will save such people apart from and, in some sense, *despite* their religion.

People Are Judged for Their Sins — Not for What They Don't Know

Whoever is judged and condemned to Hell cannot claim that their sentence is unjust. It *would* be unjust if they were condemned for failing to believe in Jesus Christ even though they had never heard of him. However, that will not be the case. The lost will be condemned not simply for failing to believe in Jesus but for their sins. God "will judge all people according to what they have done" (Rom. 2:6 NLT; see also Ps. 62:12; Prov. 24:12; Matt. 16:27; Rev. 2:23). After God raises the dead, they will be "judged according to their deeds" (Rev. 20:13 NLT).

There is a great deal of confusion on this point, even among astute theologians. Tiessen, for example, asserts, "I think that there is a basic truth that intuitively leads Christians to reject the idea that God would condemn people for not believing in one of whom they have never heard, when only that faith would save them."[5] But people who have never heard of Christ are not condemned for not believing in him. Those people who are condemned, whether they have heard of Christ or not, are condemned for their sins. If they have heard of Christ but chosen not to believe in him, that is an especially grievous sin, but not the sole basis for their condemnation.

Tiessen later admits that this is the position of those theologians whom he is criticizing; they "defend God's justice by arguing that the unevangelized are not condemned for not believing in a Jesus of whom they were ignorant but are condemned only for the sins they committed knowingly."[6] His earlier criticism, then, confused the issue.

By contrast, those who have heard of Christ and put their faith in him are saved solely by God's grace through faith (Eph. 2:8–9). Thus, while rejection of Christ is not the sole basis for a person's condemnation (and those who have never heard of Christ might still be condemned for their sins), acceptance of Christ is the sole basis for the salvation of those who accept him.

Those Who Reject the Gospel Will Be Lost

Whatever might be the outcome for people who have never heard the gospel, we are on solid ground in asserting that those who *have* heard it and who reject it will be lost. Jesus warned, "Whoever rejects me rejects the one who sent me" (Luke 10:16; similarly John 12:48). In a follow-up to the famous verse John 3:16, we read: "Whoever believes in him is not condemned, but whoever does not believe stands condemned already because he has not believed in the name of God's one and only Son" (3:18 NIV). We think this text has implications for those who have not heard the gospel, but at the very least it indicates that those who have heard the message about Jesus the Son of God and disbelieved it are under God's judgment.

The writer of Hebrews warns that those who "willfully persist in sin after having received the knowledge of the truth" have forfeited Christ's sacrifice for their sins and have "a fearful prospect of judgment" (Heb. 10:26–27). This passage is speaking specifically of people who used to profess belief in Christ and then rejected him, but the broader implication is that anyone who willfully rejects Christ is in serious trouble. The principle, once again, is that people are accountable for what they know.

Of course, it follows from the fact that Jesus is the only Savior that anyone who rejects him as Savior will be lost. If "no one comes to the Father except through" Christ (John 14:6), and we refuse to come to the Father through Christ, we simply won't be coming to the Father at all.

It's difficult to quantify how many people have heard the gospel of Jesus Christ and rejected him. Clearly, though, the number is at least in the hundreds of millions. There is no getting around this unpleasant reality: hundreds of millions of people have turned their backs on the only Savior and gone into eternity without Christ.

But what about the billions of people who have never even heard of Christ? If they haven't heard of him, surely they haven't rejected him. Will such people also be lost? Might there be some exceptions? We will consider this question in the next two chapters.

SENSE

Jesus Christ is the only Savior.

NONSENSE

Christians think they are saved by virtue of being in the right religion.

Chapter 14

IF I SHOULD
DIE BEFORE I
HEAR

Are infants and others incapable of responding to the
gospel going to Hell?

We come now to the question of the possibility of salvation for the unevangelized—those who have never heard the gospel. We have already established that those who have heard the gospel are responsible for responding to it in repentance and faith. We have also shown that however people might end up being saved, everyone who has been saved is saved through the redeeming death and resurrection of Jesus Christ. All evangelical Christians agree on these two basic points. From that initial agreement, though, opinions diverge sharply on the matter of those who have not heard the gospel of Jesus Christ.

Varieties of Exclusivism and Inclusivism

The usual and simplest way of classifying the different views on this question is to distinguish between *exclusivism* (also called *restrictivism*), which maintains that only persons who put faith consciously in Jesus Christ may be saved, and *inclusivism*, which maintains that some persons who have never heard of Jesus Christ may nevertheless be saved by him.[1] However, this simple distinction turns out to mask a considerable diversity of views. Some believe that those who have not heard the gospel from other people, but whom God knows will accept the gospel if they hear it, receive a revelation from angels, Jesus himself, or internally by the Holy Spirit during their lifetime (which we may call the *premortem revelation* view).[2] Others think that all people will encounter Jesus and be given an opportunity to respond to the gospel just at the moment of death (the *final option* view).[3] Yet another view is that those who have not heard the gospel in this life may nevertheless hear it during the intermediate state (the *postmortem evangelism* view).[4] The Mormon Church teaches a most elaborate version of this doctrine,[5] but some form of it was taught by Clement of Alexandria, Origen, Athanasius, and other church fathers, and in recent years has been defended by Gabriel Fackre.[6]

In a sense, these positions can be described as variations of exclusivism, since they agree that to be saved a person must hear about Christ and consciously put faith in him. What theologians usually mean by exclusivism, though, is the belief that people can only put faith in Jesus Christ and be saved through a human witness to the gospel during their lifetime. Terrance Tiessen calls this view *ecclesiocentrism*, since this view essentially limits salvation to those who come into contact with the church.[7] We will refer to it as *hard exclusivism*.

Inclusivism also comes in several varieties. Some hold that God saves those whom he knows would have accepted the gospel had they heard it.[8] We call this view *middle knowledge inclusivism*, because "middle knowledge" refers to knowledge of what has not happened but would have happened under different circumstances.[9] Others believe that God saves those who have never heard of Christ but who have a repentant or penitent disposition of humble faith in God, even though their knowledge about God is defective. According to this view, God saves those who respond in faith to the light that they have, even if that faith includes no knowledge about Jesus Christ. We call this view *pietistic inclusivism*, since it regards anyone who has a certain kind of piety or faith as saved.[10] Another view, *agnostic inclusivism*, maintains that God could save persons who have never heard of Jesus Christ but that we have no way of knowing if he will in fact do so.[11]

We must point out that none of these types of inclusivism commits their advocates to any opinion as to *how many* people will be saved without having heard of Jesus Christ. In general, agnostic inclusivists tend to be the most pessimistic—or at least noncommittal—but their view allows for any number of people whom God might choose to save outside of the church. But one could hold to pietistic inclusivism without concluding that the number of people saved by faith apart from conscious knowledge of Christ will be large. Thus it is not quite correct to define inclusivism as the belief "that millions of unevangelized adults" will be saved.[12] Inclusivism allows for this possibility, but only nonevangelical versions of inclusivism clearly posit the conclusion that millions of unevangelized adults will be saved.

Those Who Haven't Heard of Jesus Christ

There are actually five categories of human beings who are (usually) understood never to have heard about Jesus Christ during their mortal lifetime.

(1) *Old Testament people.* The Israelites in the Old Testament, as well as believers in God before Israel existed, did not know Jesus Christ by name. Yet we know that many of them were saved.

(2) *Young children who have died.* Unborn children, infants, and even young children cannot respond to a presentation of the gospel from other people because they can't hear or understand it. Does this mean that if they die before they can understand and respond to the gospel, they are necessarily lost?

(3) *Mentally incapable people.* Those who are incapable of processing a verbal presentation of the gospel because of mental retardation, mental illness, or other debilitating effects on the mind cannot be expected to respond to such presentations. Are they lost?

(4) *Pre-Christ heathen.* (We use the term *heathen* to refer to people who never heard of the God of the Jews or Christians, not as a term of abuse.) Most of humanity before the coming of Christ had never heard of the Lord, the God of Abraham. We may assume for the sake of argument that people exposed to God's dealings with Israel had an opportunity to repent and believe in God, but

what about the millions who had no such opportunity? What about noble pre-Christian individuals like Socrates who had no exposure to Israel and Israel's God?

(5) *Post-Christ heathen.* There have been billions of mentally capable people of responsible age living since the time of Jesus' death and resurrection who have never heard the gospel of Jesus Christ. Are all of them lost?

Human beings in all five of these categories could properly be described as "unevangelized," since (we presume) they literally have not had the gospel of Jesus Christ presented to them during their mortal lifetimes. It turns out, though, that the major disagreement is about the possibility of salvation for the pre-Christian and post-Christian heathen, as the accompanying table shows.

All seven of these views agree that at least some people will be saved among the categories of Old Testament people, children who die young, and the mentally incapable. Most of these views (both inclusivist and exclusivist) agree that some of the heathen both before and after Christ will be saved. Agnostic inclusivists think that some of the heathen may be saved, but that there is no way of telling; hard exclusivists think that none of the heathen will be saved.

In the rest of this chapter, we will examine what we can know from Scripture about the salvation of Old Testament believers as well as infants and others incapable of hearing the gospel in any era. In the next chapter, we will discuss the salvation of responsible human beings to whom believers do not take the gospel.

Old Testament Believers Will Be Saved

People living before Jesus, including Abel, Enoch, Noah, Abraham, Sarah, Isaac, Jacob, Joseph, Moses, Rahab, Samuel, David, Elijah, and an unknown number of other people are saved and will live forever in God's kingdom (Matt. 8:11; 17:3; 22:32; Luke 9:30; 13:28; 16:22–25; Rom. 4:1–7; Heb. 11:4–32). Evidently, then, it is possible for some people to be saved without having heard the name "Jesus" or the message that he died on the cross for our sins. At the very least, it *used* to be possible; and if it was possible then, *perhaps* it's possible now.

Who Will Be Saved?

	Old Testament People	Young Children	Mentally Incapables	Pre-Christ Heathen	Post-Christ Heathen
Exclusivist Views					
Premortem Revelation	some	some	some	some	some
Final Option	some	some	some	some	some
Postmortem Evangelism	some	some	some	some	some
Hard Exclusivism	some	some/all	some/all	none	none
Inclusivist Views					
Middle Knowledge	some	some	some	some	some
Pietistic	some	some	some/all	some	some
Agnostic	some	some/all	some/all	unknown	unknown

Some hard exclusivists disagree. Ronald Nash, for example, states, "The New Testament reports that the Old Testament saints looked forward to a mediator who would die (Jn 5:46; 8:56; 1 Pet 1:10–12) and says that the gospel was preached to Abraham (Gal 3:6)."[13] In response, we should note first of all that Nash's texts from John say nothing about the mediator (Jesus) dying.

It is true that according to Peter, the Old Testament prophets were curious to understand "what person or time the Spirit of Christ within them was indicating as He predicted the sufferings of Christ and the glories to follow" (1 Pet. 1:11 NASB), but these prophets came toward the end of the Old Testament era. Thus, his statement does not support the idea that everyone who was saved in the Old Testament believed in a coming Messiah who would die for our sins. Moreover, Peter says that those prophets "were serving not themselves but you" (1 Pet. 1:12). That statement clearly implies that the prophets' revelations about the Messiah were not given as knowledge that Old Testament believers had to know in order to be saved. Rather, they were advance notices that prepared the way for the Messiah to be recognized after he had come, died, and risen again.

As far as we can tell, few if any Jews before Jesus' death and resurrection knew that the Messiah was going to die for their sins. The first Old Testament passage that we think can be shown in context to teach that the Messiah was going to die for our sins is Isaiah 52:13–53:12, the famous passage about the Suffering Servant.[14] However, apparently few if any Jews understood this before Jesus, and of course Isaiah 53 was written hundreds of years after many of the Old Testament saints had died (the patriarchs, Moses, David, Elijah, etc.). Other passages lay the groundwork for the unfolding revelation of the coming Messiah and his sacrificial work but stop short of an explicit or clear enunciation of the doctrine that the Messiah would die to atone for our sins (e.g., Gen. 3:15; 22:8; Ps. 22:1–18). Moreover—and this is the critical point—*none of these passages suggests that belief in the Messiah's future redemptive death was necessary for salvation.*

Nash does have a point, however. The gospel was there in the Old Testament, at least in germinal form. Paul says as much: "And the scripture, foreseeing that God would justify the Gentiles by faith, declared the gospel beforehand to Abraham, saying, 'All the Gentiles shall be blessed in you'" (Gal. 3:8). Paul is here referring to God's repeated promise to Abraham that all the families or nations of the earth would be blessed through him (Gen. 12:3; 18:18; 22:18). He goes on to argue that the promised blessing to the earth's peoples would come through Abraham's "offspring," the Messiah (Gal. 3:14, 16). Paul nowhere suggests that Abraham understood that the Messiah would bring this worldwide blessing by dying for our sins. It was enough that "Abraham 'believed God, and it was reckoned to him as righteousness'" (Gal. 3:6, quoting Gen. 15:6). What Abraham believed was that somehow God would give him a son through whom his promises of land, progeny, and blessing to the world would be fulfilled (Gen. 12:1–3; 13:14–17; 15:1–7, 18–21; 17:1–8; 18:17–18; 22:17–18).

People in the Old Testament were saved, then, without knowing about Jesus or his redemptive death. Still, we should be cautious against making too much of this fact. By no means does the Bible suggest that everyone or even most people before Jesus were saved. It doesn't even encourage us to think that most Israelites were saved; in fact, we know that many were not (e.g., Rom. 9:6–8; 1 Cor. 10:5). And those non-Israelites whose salvation we know anything about were believers in the Lord God, not in any of the gods and goddesses of the ancient pagan nations.

The few apparent examples of individuals not physically related to Abraham who were saved in the Old Testament era had ties to Abraham or his descendants. Melchizedek is the most significant example; although not related to Abram (as he was then known), "he was priest of God Most High" (Heb. *El Elyon*), acknowledging Abram's God as the true God (Gen. 14:18–20). We have no information as to how Melchizedek came to worship the same God as Abram. Bryan Widbin suggests that Melchizedek received a revelation from God independent of Abram:

Abram lived on the fringe of Canaanite society with a different cultural orientation than that of the city-states (Gen. 13). Are we not to assume that Abram and Melchizedek came by their knowledge of El Elyon independently, perhaps through their distinct revelations of God?[15]

Widbin may be right, but we don't have enough information to be sure. What is certain is that Melchizedek was not a devout pagan. He worshiped the same God as Abram.

Job and the men who converse with him are sometimes cited as examples of saved non-Israelites. Job lived in Uz (Job 1:1) and Elihu, the young man who challenged Job, is described as the "son of Barachel the Buzite, of the family of Ram" (32:2). Buz and Uz were both names of sons of Nahor, Abraham's brother (Gen. 22:20–21). This suggests that Elihu and Job may actually have been related to Abraham. In any case, they worshiped the same God. Naturally, the Old Testament has little information about the salvation of people who had no contact with Abraham or his descendants, so we should also not make much of the lack of such information.

Infants and Incapables

Our second and third categories of "unevangelized" people are children who die before they could possibly hear or respond to the gospel and mentally incapable people of whatever age who also lack the capacity to listen and respond to the gospel. What about them?

All Christians agree that *at least some* of the human beings in these two categories will be saved, and many Christians think that *all* of them will be. The primary question here is not whether infants and incapables can consciously believe in Christ in order to be saved, but whether they can commit sins in order to be damned. As others have argued, we would say that they cannot commit sins deserving condemnation and therefore will all be saved. Here we are in agreement with Ronald Nash, among others.[16] The argument may be summarized as follows:

- God will judge people and condemn them on the basis of their sinful works (Ps. 62:12; Prov. 24:12; Matt. 16:27; Rom. 2:6; 2 Cor. 5:10; Rev. 2:23; 20:13; see ch. 13).
- Unborn children, infants, and the mentally incapable are incapable of doing either good or evil (Deut. 1:39; Isa.

7:15–16; Rom. 9:11) and therefore cannot do anything deserving of condemnation.

- Therefore, no unborn children, infants, or mentally incapable people will be condemned.

Not all evangelical Christians have embraced this line of reasoning. We are aware of four objections to its conclusion.[17] (1) Scripture does not actually state the conclusion of the argument; it does not say that all infants (for example) will be saved. This objection (which is essentially an argument from silence) loses its force once we recognize that the two premises of the argument are both biblical and the conclusion clearly follows from those premises.

(2) Scripture teaches that all people are conceived and born with the fallen, sinful condition of humankind and that Adam's guilt is "imputed" or "reckoned" to the entire human race (Rom. 5:12–19; Ps. 51:5; cf. Eph. 2:3). True enough, but what this proves is not that some (or all) infants who die will be lost but that infants who will be saved need to be redeemed from the Adamic curse. The proper conclusion would seem to be that God will somehow regenerate these people and save them despite their lack of any capacity to hear and respond to the gospel.

(3) The idea of all infants being chosen by God for salvation, but not all adults, is said to be contrary to his impartiality. This objection has things precisely backward: it is because God is impartial that he will save anyone and everyone who has not personally done anything wrong.

(4) It has been urged that Scripture disallows the idea that God would choose anyone for salvation based on works, yet choosing to save infants and incapables because they have done nothing wrong is a form of salvation by works. This objection fails for the same reason as the previous objection: salvation by works is impossible for

JOHN MACARTHUR

It is the sins that sinners commit that constitute the record that is established against them, by which condemnation falls from the throne of God. Little children don't have that record.[18]

mentally competent human beings because all of them have committed sinful works. Furthermore, it is by God's grace that infants and the other incompetents are saved from the Adamic curse and given eternal life, because these humans cannot do anything *good* to merit salvation, either (cf. Rom. 9:11). Thus, incompetents are not saved by works, because they have none to contribute.

Although we are not dogmatic in this matter, we do think the argument for believing that God will save all human beings who lack the capacity to commit sin as a result of mental incapacity (the unborn, infants, and incapables) is strong. Ironically, some of the leading evangelical critics of this conclusion are inclusivists. Both John Sanders and Terrance Tiessen assert that evangelicals who affirm that all infants and other incompetents will be saved do so based on "extrabiblical beliefs" and for "sentimental reasons."[19] Yet hard exclusivists make these same criticisms of inclusivism.

If it is true that all children who die in the womb or in infancy will be saved, along with all those with mental incapacities, the implications for the population of Heaven is staggering. Considering the rates for miscarriages, stillborn deaths, and infant mortality for most of human history (and even today), the number of such children whom we may expect to live forever in God's kingdom will conservatively be in the billions. They might even end up outnumbering the responsible older children and adults who are saved through their faith.

SENSE

God will save all who die in infancy and others incapable of moral evil.

NONSENSE

Only persons who explicitly believe in Christ will be saved.

Chapter 15

NO HEAVEN FOR THE HEATHEN?

Salvation for people who have never heard of Christ is
the exception, not the rule.

Whether some or all persons in the categories of children
dying in the womb or in infancy and the mentally incapable
will be saved, the salvation of *any* such persons poses a significant
question. If God can save such persons apart from any conscious,
explicit knowledge and affirmation of the gospel or of any truth
about God at all, does this not falsify hard exclusivism? That is,
doesn't the salvation of these people prove that some people are
in fact saved apart from knowing and affirming any revelation of
God's redemptive purpose in Christ?

In posing this question, we are absolutely *not* equating the
inability of the heathen with the inability of infants and the mentally incapable. Responsible adults (and older children) who have
never heard the gospel are all confirmed sinners, guilty of sinful
deeds, for which God would be just to hold each and every one of
them eternally accountable. Thus, God would be perfectly just in
consigning all of them to Hell. For that matter, he would be perfectly just to consign all of *us* to Hell, too. That he chooses to show
any of us mercy is wonderful; no one has any grounds for complaint if God doesn't choose to extend this mercy to every sinner in
human history (Rom. 9:14–22).

No, the issue is not whether God must save the heathen. He is under no obligation to do so. The issue is whether God *might* save *some* of the heathen even if they never receive a human witness to the gospel during their mortal lifetimes. If he can regenerate infants and the mentally incapable apart from knowledge of the gospel, might he not be able to do so for some of the heathen?

To answer this question, we must consider whether any of the proposed explanations of how God might save the unevangelized are biblically plausible.

Revelations of a Lifetime

The premortem revelation position asserts that God sometimes conveys special revelations through angels, an internal work of the Holy Spirit, or perhaps a vision of Jesus to individuals cut off from the church's witness. We see no biblical obstacle to this claim as long as such special revelations are not regarded as authoritative for the church. However, there does not seem to be any biblical basis for this claim, which seems to be based on anecdotal evidence.[1] It is sometimes suggested that the Magi who traveled to Jerusalem looking for the King of the Jews (Matt. 2:1–2) are an example of such a revelation, but the fact that they knew about the Jews and their hope of a King is better explained on the supposition that the Magi had access to at least some biblical knowledge (even if secondhand).

The fact that Jesus instructed his disciples to spread the gospel by taking it themselves to all the nations (Matt. 24:14; 28:19; Luke 24:47; Acts 1:8) surely implies at the very least that such human witness was to be the normal, usual, common way for non-Jewish (as well as Jewish)[2] people to hear the gospel. The New Testament consistently characterizes the Gentile nations as shrouded in darkness and futility of mind (Acts 26:18; Rom. 1:21–23; Eph. 4:17–18), "having no hope and without God in the world" (Eph. 2:12). That characterization likewise requires us to view any premortem revelations to individuals among the heathen as at best exceptional, not routine or common.

At-Death Encounters with Jesus

The suggestion that all people will encounter Jesus and be given an opportunity to respond to the gospel at the moment of death does not appear to have any biblical basis. Tiessen, who advocates a form of this view, admits that "the proposal that we all meet Christ at death moves us beyond Scripture's explicit teaching into the speculative." In fact, he offers no biblical support, explicit or implicit, for the idea.[3]

Although Tiessen claims that the idea is consistent with Scripture (which perhaps it is), it really does nothing to solve the problem of the salvation of the unevangelized. Why not? Because in Tiessen's view, the unevangelized are not converted, or brought from condemnation to salvation, through this encounter with Jesus at death. Rather, their relationship to God has *already* been set by their choices in life either to believe and trust in God and hope in his grace or to follow a different path. Those heathen who are saved despite never having heard a human witness to Christ are saved by their faith, *prior to* their dying encounter with Christ.[4] So what is the point of the at-death meeting with Jesus? Apparently its function is to satisfy hard exclusivists that any heathen that might be saved will put explicit faith in Jesus before dying. In other words, the final option, at least as Tiessen presents it, appears to have polemical value but no theological value as a way of explaining how the unevangelized can be saved.

Saved by Responding in Faith to the Light Available

Tiessen's version of the final option presupposes the pietistic variety of inclusivism, according to which God saves those who have never heard of Christ but who have a repentant or penitent disposition of humble faith in God. The theory is that God holds people responsible only for responding to the light that they have, and therefore anyone who responds in faith to the light of God's revelation in nature, conscience, or the occasional extraordinary means will be saved. Among evangelicals, this may be the most popular alternative to hard exclusivism.

What we said earlier about the presumption created by New Testament teaching that the non-Jewish nations are in spiritual darkness applies here. Those nations were in darkness because their people, in general if not without exception, failed to respond in faith to the light they had. At most the theory of salvation by the available light offers an exceptional, out-of-the-norm way that God might save some people who have never heard of Christ. We would be talking about a few candles here and there in a vast land of darkness — and that is the best-case scenario.

Hard exclusivists go further and preclude the possibility of a relatively small number of people being saved in this way. We are unclear as to the biblical basis for dogmatically viewing such salvation as impossible. It is true, of course, that no one among the heathen lives up to *all* of the light that they have: "since all have sinned" (Rom. 3:23), whether they have God's revelation in Scripture or not (cf. 2:12–16). There is no possibility of noble heathen being saved by their good works.[5] Then again, Christians do not live up to the light they have, either.

> The nations were in darkness because their people, in general if not without exception, failed to respond in faith to the light they had.

The matter needs to be refocused. Could persons who have never heard the gospel come to understand that God is their Creator, that they have sinned against him, and that they should throw themselves on his mercy? We think they could. God's revelation of himself in nature demonstrates him to be not only great in power, wisdom, glory, and goodness, but also to be merciful and kind, sending blessing on both good and bad people (Ps. 19:1–6; Matt. 5:45; Acts 14:15–17; Rom. 1:20). The Holy Spirit would need to illuminate their minds to perceive these truths about God, but then again, he needs to do that in order to save us as well.

God Knows That They Would Have Believed

The middle-knowledge explanation for salvation of the unevangelized also has no clear biblical support for it. That God has middle knowledge may be granted, at least for the sake of argument; that he chooses to save people who never heard the gospel on the basis of his middle knowledge that they would have repented and believed if they had heard the gospel is speculation.

The middle knowledge form of inclusivism also suffers from a problem similar to the final option theory. Suppose God does know that a certain unevangelized person would have believed if she had heard the gospel. A reasonable question to ask is whether the way she lived her actual life reflected that fact in God's middle knowledge. It doesn't make any sense to say that a person who would have believed in Christ if given the opportunity would live in precisely the same way as a person in the same situation who would not have believed if given the same opportunity. Suppose, then, we answer that the way such a person lived her actual life would in some way reflect the fact that if given the opportunity she would have believed in Christ. Since salvation is a gift of God's grace, not a matter of works, what would be different about her would be an attitude—presumably one akin to faith with humble dependence on God and his mercy.

In short, the middle knowledge explanation seems to require the pietistic explanation that those persons will be saved who respond to the light by trusting in God and his grace as best they understand. Surely someone who would have believed in Christ if given the opportunity would also respond to whatever light concerning God's grace he or she did have opportunity to receive.

Therefore, the middle knowledge version of inclusivism, like the final option view, cannot stand alone as a rationale for the salvation of the unevangelized, but presupposes the pietistic form of inclusivism.

Hearing the Gospel after Death

Probably the least popular view among evangelicals of the unevangelized is the idea that after they die, they will hear the gospel and be given an opportunity to repent and believe. Gabriel Fackre, cited earlier, is conspicuously exceptional as an evangelical favoring this view. It is, of course, the official teaching of the Mormons, for whom the idea is central to their religion. Mormons practice baptisms for the dead because they believe that the dead for whom they are baptized will then have the opportunity to accept the Mormon gospel and eventually become exalted to the celestial kingdom (the highest level in eternity in Mormon theology). Whether in its Mormon form or not, more is at stake with this theory than with any of the others we are considering because it suggests that most of the people who will convert to faith in Christ will do so after death. We must therefore take a closer look at this doctrine.

Ironically, while the other views we have been considering generally are not claimed to be explicitly affirmed in Scripture, advocates of the postmortem evangelism view do make that claim. They base their biblical case almost entirely on two statements in 1 Peter. We will quote a good bit of the passage, but you should read it in its entirety (and in more than one translation, if possible):

> For Christ also died for sins once for all, righteous for unrighteous people, so that he might bring us to God, having been put to death in the flesh but having been made alive in the spirit, *in which also he went and made proclamation to the spirits in prison*, who once were disobedient, when the patience of God was waiting in the days of Noah, during the construction of the ark, in which a few, that is, eight souls, were brought safely through water. (1 Pet. 3:18–20, translation ours)

> For enough time has already passed doing the desire of the Gentiles ... but they will give account to the one who is ready to judge the living and the dead. For *this purpose the gospel was preached even to the dead*, that though they are judged in the flesh according to men, they may live in the spirit according to God. (1 Pet. 4:3–6, translation ours)[6]

Understandably, Peter's statement that "the gospel was preached even to the dead" (4:6) has been understood to refer to an opportunity after death to hear the gospel and be saved. The "proclamation to the spirits in prison" (3:19) has been understood in the same way. However, a careful study of this passage in context shows that Peter has something else in mind in these statements.

Throughout the epistle Peter makes it clear that a person's eternal future is determined in this life. He encourages Gentile Christians to persevere in faith despite various trials, with the outcome being their salvation (1 Pet. 1:6–9). Because God judges people according to their work, they should conduct themselves "in reverent fear" during their life here and now (1:17). Unfortunately, non-Christians may be expected to slander the Christians as evildoers and treat them harshly even though they are not doing anything wrong (2:12, 19–20).

Believers are to follow Christ's example and keep trusting in God while suffering (1 Pet. 2:21–23). If they suffer for the sake of righteousness, they should consider themselves blessed and continue keeping a good conscience (3:14–17). After all, Christ suffered death in the flesh at the hands of persecutors, but God exalted him (3:18–22); Christians should therefore be prepared to suffer death at the hands of their persecutors (4:1). They should not be surprised at such persecution, but rejoice that they are sharing in Christ's suffering as a Christian and entrust themselves to God's will (4:12–16). By humbling themselves now, they can look forward to God's exalting them when the time comes (5:6–10).

It would be strange, in the context of all this emphatic teaching about the necessity of persevering in faith and holy living through trials and suffering, if Peter were to state as an aside that those who never heard the gospel will get a chance to be saved after death. The natural question Peter's readers would have asked, had Peter really said that, was why they themselves couldn't have been given such a sweet deal!

The theory that Peter was referring to a proclamation of the gospel to departed spirits as an invitation to salvation assumes that "the spirits in prison" (1 Pet. 3:19) were part or all of "the dead" (4:6). This assumption is almost certainly incorrect, as a comparison of the two parts of the epistle demonstrates.

In these two paragraphs or units of the epistle, there is a close parallel, but it is between Christ and those who had the gospel preached to them: both were unjustly killed in the flesh but live in the spirit. The parallel is *not* between "the spirits in prison" of

1 Peter 3:18–22	1 Peter 4:1–6
Christ ... put to death in the flesh ... made alive in the spirit	The dead ... judged in the flesh ... may live in the spirit
Christ made the proclamation (*ekēruxen*)	Unnamed person(s) preached the gospel (*euēngelisthē*)
Proclamation "to the spirits in prison, who disobeyed"	Preaching the gospel "to the dead" (who will "live according to God")
The spirits disobeyed "in the days of Noah"	No context in the Old Testament past

3:19 and "the dead" of 4:6. They are described in two different ways: what they hear is expressed differently (proclamation in 3:19, preaching the gospel in 4:6), the one making the proclamation in 3:19 is identified as Christ but 4:6 does not say who preached the gospel, the spirits in 3:19 are from the time of Noah but the dead in 4:6 apparently are not, and the spirits are characterized as disobedient while the dead in 4:6 are not (in fact they will "live ... according to God").[7]

For these (and other) reasons, few New Testament scholars today think that 1 Peter 3–4 teaches an opportunity for salvation after death. Peter's statement in 4:6 does not mean that after people die they get the gospel preached to them. We can be reasonably sure this is not what Peter meant because what he says is not "the gospel is preached" but "the gospel *was* preached." Rather, Peter is saying that the gospel was preached to people who had since died as a result of persecution for Christ's sake.[8] Those people whom the worldly authorities had judged worthy of physical death were nevertheless living spiritually in God's care.

Such an assurance fits the context perfectly: Peter is letting his Christian readers know that their departed fellow believers are not lost and that, whatever happens to them, God also promises them life in the spirit. Christians toward the end of the apostolic generation were concerned about the fate of their brothers and sisters who had died (cf. 1 Thess. 4:13–18), and in this context Peter's remarks are very apropos.

What about those "spirits in prison"? The interpretation of 1 Peter 3:19 remains a highly controversial matter. Although numerous explanations have been given, two major views may be considered serious options.

The older view, first suggested tentatively by the church father Augustine, is that Peter means that Christ in his preexistent state as divine spirit proclaimed a message of repentance and judgment through Noah before the Flood. In other words, "he made proclamation to the spirits in prison" means that he made this proclamation through Noah to human beings who are now (from Peter's perspective) spirits in prison. Peter's statement earlier in the same epistle that "the Spirit of Christ" was speaking through the Old Testament prophets (1 Pet. 1:11) shows that Peter could speak in this way.[9]

Although Augustine's view remains a serious option and has able defenders, the view that dominates modern scholarship is that Christ after his death (or even after his resurrection) proclaimed victory over the fallen angels who had sinned in the days of Noah. This proclamation is then an assertion of Christ's exaltation over all spiritual powers, a point made in the immediate context (1 Pet. 3:22). The same subject of those wicked angelic spirits comes up in 2 Peter 2:4–5 and Jude 6.[10]

Either one of these two views fits the general subject matter of 1 Peter and is consistent with the rest of the New Testament. The view that Christ preached the gospel in the spirit realm to give dead people an opportunity to repent and be saved does not fit the context of 1 Peter or the details of the passage. It also disagrees with the New Testament teaching that a person's eternal future is decided in this life: "People are appointed to die once, and then to face judgment" (Heb. 9:27 NET). Death is literally a dead end with regard to repentance. For that reason, Christians should reject the theory of postmortem evangelism.

A Balancing Act

A Christian view of the fate of the unevangelized masses of humanity who have lived and died without hearing the gospel must balance several clear biblical truths.

(1) First and foremost, we must recognize that the Great Commission—Jesus' standing orders to his people until his glorious return—presumes that "the nations," from whose people we are to "make disciples" (Matt. 28:19), are at least *in general* lost in spiritual darkness and in need of salvation. The message is to be one of "repentance and forgiveness of sins" and is to "be proclaimed in his name to all the nations" (Luke 24:47).

When the Jerusalem believers heard Peter's report of his visit to the household of the Roman centurion Cornelius, their response was to say, "Then God has given even to the Gentiles the repentance that leads to life" (Acts 11:18). Paul understood his mission to the Gentiles in the same way: "to open their eyes so that they may turn from darkness to light and from the dominion of Satan to God, that they may receive forgiveness of sins and an inheritance among those who have been sanctified by faith in Me" (26:18 NASB). This statement presupposes that the Gentiles are in darkness, under the dominion of Satan, alienated from God by their sins, and excluded from the inheritance of God's children (see also Eph. 2:12; Col. 1:12–13). The gospel, according to Paul, "is the power of God for salvation to everyone who has faith, to the Jew first and also to the Greek" (Rom. 1:16).

(2) We have solid reasons to think that God can and will save many people through Jesus Christ as their Savior even though they have never heard of him or of his sacrificial death on the cross for their salvation. We have seen that it is most likely the case that all of the billions of children who die before birth or in infancy will be saved. We expect the same to be true for the unknown but presumably sizable number of people whose mental capacities are so limited that they are incapable of doing good or evil.

Furthermore, believers in the Old Testament had varying degrees of understanding of his redemptive purposes and plan, few if any knew that the Messiah was going to die for their sins, and yet God saved them on the basis of that redemptive death through their humble reliance on his mercy and love. Undoubtedly the light of God's revelation to those Old Testament saints was far brighter than any light he shone elsewhere; yet it was a comparatively weak and dim light next to Jesus Christ, "the light of the world" (John 8:12). Still, God saved those believers through that light before the Light. It does not seem impossible that he might do the same for some who had no contact with Abraham and his descendants.

(3) There is no clear biblical teaching or biblically based argument that provides a sure basis or explanation for how God might save (non-infantile) people who have never been exposed to the gospel or even to its revealed anticipation in the Old Testament. The doctrine that people who never heard the gospel in their lifetime hear it in the afterlife is unbiblical. The suggestion that Jesus, angels, or the Holy Spirit reveals the gospel to isolated individuals among the unevangelized nations has no real biblical support and relies on anecdotal evidence; it is possible but likely to be rare.

The theory of universal appearances of Jesus to human beings at the moment of their death doesn't really explain how anyone is saved. The theory that God saves those whom he knows (by his "middle knowledge") would have repented and believed if they had heard the gospel also doesn't work as a complete explanation. Both of these theories require the idea that God saves those who have an implicit or rudimentary faith in God despite not having any knowledge of the biblical revelation or the gospel. This theory seems the most promising, yet at best it also can only indicate the possibility of salvation for a small minority of people in unevangelized nations. We think J. I. Packer struck a fine balance regarding the possibility of such people being saved:

> In heaven, any such penitents will learn that they were saved by Christ's death and their hearts were renewed by the Holy Spirit, and they will worship God accordingly. Christians since the second century have voiced the hope that there are such people, and we may properly voice the same hope today. But—and this is the point to consider—we have no warrant from Scripture to expect

that God will act thus in any single case where the Gospel is not yet known. To cherish this hope, therefore, is not to diminish in the slightest our urgent and never-ending missionary obligation, any more than it is to embrace universalism as a basis for personal and communal living. Living by the Bible means assuming that no one will be saved apart from faith in Christ, and acting accordingly.[11]

We conclude that a responsible position for Christians to take is that the (non-infantile) people of unevangelized nations past and present are *for the most part* lost and under divine condemnation. Our presumption should be that God's purpose is to save people from all nations *primarily* through the church's evangelistic witness. In short, we should assume that people who have never heard the gospel need it in order to be saved, while also acknowledging that God may very well have found a way to save some people apart from the human preaching of the gospel.

SENSE

We should take the gospel to all people as if their lives depended on it.

NONSENSE

We know that no one whom we fail to reach will be saved.

Chapter 16

MOVIN' ON UP!

More than one religion thinks that we will be divided
into different domains for eternity.

The traditional belief that all human beings will eventually
spend eternity either in Heaven or Hell does not satisfy everyone. Various religious groups arising out of a Christian background
in the past couple of centuries have developed more complicated
views of the eternal state for the redeemed. We will consider the
beliefs about Heaven of two of these groups, the Mormons and the
Jehovah's Witnesses.

Latter-day Saints: Three Heavenly Kingdoms

The religion best known for the view that there are multiple heavens is The Church of Jesus Christ of Latter-day Saints (the LDS,
also known as the Mormons). The LDS Church teaches that there
are three heavenly "kingdoms" where most human beings will be
distributed at the final judgment. The "celestial kingdom" is the
highest heaven, where God and Jesus live and where good Mormons
hope to go. The "terrestrial kingdom" is a heavenly realm for decent
people who were not good Mormons. The "telestial kingdom" will
be the heavenly home of the spiritual riff-raff who wouldn't even
accept the Mormon gospel when it was presented to them in the
afterlife.[1]

Joseph Smith, the founder of Mormonism, attempted to support his doctrine of three different heavenly "kingdoms" by appeals to the Bible—though usually not the Bible as it has been preserved. Compare, for example, 1 Corinthians 15:40 in the KJV and in the so-called Joseph Smith Translation:

1 Corinthians 15:40 KJV	1 Corinthians 15:40 Joseph Smith Translation
There are also celestial bodies, and bodies terrestrial: but the glory of the celestial *is* one, and the *glory* of the terrestrial *is* another.	Also celestial bodies, and bodies terrestrial, **and bodies telestial**; but the glory of the celestial, one, and the terrestrial, another, **and the telestial, another.**

Smith omitted the words italicized in the KJV (which is fine, since they were added to complete the sense in English), but then he added two whole phrases in order to introduce into the passage the third of his three eternal kingdoms, the so-called "telestial" kingdom. Smith appears to have coined the word *telestial* by combining the words *terrestrial* and *celestial*. Adding these phrases is not only unjustified textually (there is, of course, no surviving Greek or other ancient manuscript of the passage containing these phrases), but it changes the whole point of the passage.

Paul is actually comparing the "glory" of heavenly and earthly bodies (the English words "celestial" and "terrestrial" mean heavenly and earthly respectively, and translate the Greek words having that meaning, *epiouranios* and *epigeios*). The term "terrestrial body" simply means any "body" down here on Earth, while a "celestial body" is any "body" up in heaven, that is, in the sky. We know this because Paul goes on immediately to mention three kinds of heavenly bodies: the sun, moon, and stars (1 Cor. 15:41). All of this is merely the development of analogies from the different kinds of objects in the natural realm to establish the principle that the resurrected human body will be different and more glorious than in its mortal state. So, after finishing his comments about the varying glory of earthly and heavenly bodies, Paul concludes: "So also is the resurrection of the dead" (v. 42 NASB).

In 2 Corinthians 12:2 Paul describes an experience of being "caught up to the third heaven," which he also identifies as "Paradise" (v. 4). Not surprisingly, Mormons cite this passage as proof that there are three spiritual heavens. However, there are some good reasons not to follow their interpretation here.

(1) Paul says nothing to explain in what sense Paradise is a "third heaven." According to one plausible interpretation, "the 'first heaven' would be atmospheric heaven (the sky) and 'second heaven' the more distant stars and planets, and therefore the 'third heaven' would refer to the place where God dwells."[2] This explanation does not introduce different spiritual heavens into the Bible, for which there is no other evidence.

(2) Paul contradicts the LDS view of the afterlife when he identifies the third heaven with Paradise: "I know a person in Christ who fourteen years ago was caught up to the third heaven.... And I know that such a person—whether in the body or out of the body I do not know, God knows—was caught up into Paradise" (2 Cor. 12:2b–4a). LDS theology, however, distinguishes Paradise—as an intermediary spiritual realm for the righteous awaiting exaltation—from the celestial kingdom, or "third heaven" in their view, as the final dwelling place of the exalted.

(3) Nowhere in the Bible is there any support for the belief in three separate heavenly kingdoms along with a fourth kingdom of Hell. The consistent teaching of Scripture is that human beings have two possible ultimate destinations, not four. Jesus divided humanity into the righteous and the wicked and assigned them to two different futures: eternal punishment and eternal life (Matt. 5:45; 25:46). In the book of Revelation, these two destinations are called "the lake of fire" (Rev. 19:20; 20:10, 14–15) and "a new heaven and a new earth" (Rev. 21:1). The Bible divides the resurrected into those condemned to eternal punishment and those promised eternal life (Dan. 12:2; John 5:28–29; Acts 24:15).

The number of biblical passages dividing humanity into two categories—the righteous and the wicked (or unrighteous), the believing and the unbelieving, those who will be saved and those who will perish—is too great to try to list them (in addition to those already mentioned, see Ps. 1:5–6; Prov. 3:33; 10:16; John 20:27; 1 Cor. 1:18; 2 Cor. 6:15). One is either a subject of Satan's domain of darkness or a subject of the kingdom of God ruled by his Son, Jesus Christ (Acts 26:18; Col. 1:13).

Jehovah's Witnesses: 144,000 in Heaven Ruling over Paradise Earth

Jehovah's Witnesses also divide the eternal state into more than one realm. Their doctrine assigns the redeemed forever to two different realms: Heaven and Earth. The vast majority of saved humanity, called the "other sheep" (John 10:16), will live forever on Earth as human beings, which will be renovated throughout the Millennium into a Paradise. This group of "other sheep" will include a "great crowd" (Rev. 7:9 NWT) of people who will never die because they will be alive when the New World begins.

According to Jehovah's Witnesses, "millions" belonging to this great crowd are living today. The rest of the "other sheep" will be resurrected to live on the Earth during the Millennium. All of these other sheep will have to prove themselves faithful and worthy during the Millennium in order to be assured of everlasting life. A comparatively small contingent of saved people called the "anointed class" or the "little flock" (cf. Luke 12:32), numbering 144,000 (Rev. 7:4–8; 14:1–5), will live forever in Heaven as spirits. The Witnesses argue that this number must be literal because it stands in contrast to the uncountable number of people in the "great crowd" (7:4, 9).[3]

Much of what the New Testament says applies only to the 144,000, according to Jehovah's Witness doctrine. Only members of the "anointed class" are permitted to partake of the elements in the Memorial, the Jehovah's Witnesses' annual observance of the Lord's Supper.[4] Only the anointed are considered "participants" in the new covenant; members of the great crowd or other sheep are "beneficiaries" but not participants in that new covenant.[5] Only the 144,000 are "born again" (John 3:3, 5; 1 Pet. 1:3). They alone are the "holy ones" ("saints" in most English Bibles, e.g., 1 Cor. 1:2); they alone are Christ's "brothers" (e.g., in Rom. 8:29) and members of the "Christian congregation" (the Jehovah's Witnesses' term for the church).

Of course, the New Testament writers routinely speak as though all believers in Christ are members of the church, participants in the new covenant, and so forth; the Witnesses' explanation is that during the first century all believers in Christ were members of the anointed class. Jehovah's Witnesses believe that essentially all of the 144,000 had already been chosen by the mid–1930s, so that by now only a few thousand remain alive.[6]

The division of Christian believers into a "little flock" and a larger company of "other sheep" is based on a misreading of two passages in the Gospels. On one occasion Jesus told his disciples, "Do not be afraid, little flock, for your Father has chosen gladly to give you the kingdom" (Luke 12:32). Jehovah's Witnesses interpret the expression "little flock" as if it were contrasting with a larger flock, but there is nothing to support this supposition in the context. The band of Jesus' disciples was at that time indeed a "little flock," a small contingent of disciples representing a small minority of the Jews living at that time. The immediately preceding verse makes it clear that those to whom the Father has chosen to give the kingdom are Jesus' disciples who seek that kingdom (v. 31).

The other misunderstood text is Jesus' statement, "I have other sheep that do not belong to this fold. I must bring them also, and they will listen to my voice. So there will be one flock, one shepherd" (John 10:16). These "other sheep" are not an earthly class of believers in contrast to a heavenly class. Rather, in the historical setting of Jesus' ministry, these "other sheep" are Gentiles who will come to faith in Jesus and be joined to his Jewish followers as a single "flock."

The other significant biblical texts used to support the doctrine of the two classes of Christians are found in the book of Revelation, the only book to use the number 144,000 (Rev. 7:4; 14:1, 3). Revelation uses many symbolic numbers (e.g., the seven spirits before the throne; the seven horns and seven eyes of the Lamb). Most telling are the symbolic dimensions of the New Jerusalem, 12,000 stadia in length, width, and height, with a wall 144 cubits high (21:16–17). As we will explain in more detail in the next chapter, we know these dimensions are symbolic because the city is not a literal cube city but an apocalyptic vision picturing the church, "the wife of the Lamb" (see Rev. 21:2, 9).

The use of the numbers 12,000 and 144 in Revelation 21 in a symbolic way strongly suggests that the similar numbers 12,000 and 144,000 in Revelation 7 are also symbolic. This makes especially good sense if one takes the 144,000 to be a symbolic picture of the church—for then these similar numbers in both sets of visions are employed with reference to the church. And as a matter of fact, Jehovah's Witnesses do take the visions of the 144,000 to symbolize the church (the "Christian congregation"). So it would seem that they ought to take the number 144,000 symbolically.

Yet they don't. Jehovah's Witnesses insist on taking the one number 144,000 in Revelation 7:4 literally. But they do not take literally the twelve numbers of 12,000 each in 7:5–8 used to add up to the 144,000. There is no exegetical or hermeneutical sense to taking the one number literally but not the twelve numbers that the same text adds together to get the one number. Jehovah's Witnesses also do not take the tribes of Israel literally. They don't take the seals literally. In Revelation 14:1–5, they don't take the Lamb or Mount Zion literally, the four living creatures literally, or the virginal status of the 144,000 literally. Yet they take the number 144,000 literally and use it to come up with a doctrine foreign to the entire New Testament.

Given the Jehovah's Witnesses' doctrinal view of taking the twelve occurrences of the number 12,000 symbolically (which add up to the 144,000), and their acknowledgment of numerous other symbolic elements in the two visions that mention the number 144,000, it seems that we have every reason to conclude that Jehovah's Witnesses, to be consistent, ought to take the number 144,000 symbolically.

Some evangelicals, be it noted, regard the number 144,000 as a literal number. However, these evangelicals take the twelve occurrences of 12,000 literally, and they take the text literally when it describes the 144,000 as people from the twelve tribes of Israel. We don't think this is the best interpretation of Revelation 7, but it is far more consistent and plausible than the Jehovah's Witnesses' view.

The main exegetical argument Jehovah's Witnesses proffer for construing the number 144,000 literally is that the number 144,000 is meant to be contrasted with the statement in the next vision about "a great multitude that no one could count" (Rev. 7:9). They argue that this statement implies that the number 144,000 is literal, because it is countable. But these are two complementary visions of the same people. Revelation 7:9 describes the great multitude as "standing before the throne and before the Lamb, robed in white." That puts the "great crowd" in Heaven! The phrase "before the throne" is the same phrase used of the 144,000 in the later vision (14:3) and always pictures the location as Heaven (1:4; 4:5, 6, 10; 7:9, 11, 15; 8:3; 14:3; 20:12).

Seen in this light, the two numerical descriptions are complementary: the number 144,000 symbolizes completeness and the church's status as a kind of spiritual Israel; the description of the multitude as beyond human enumeration emphasizes the vastness of the company of the redeemed. Therefore, the juxtaposition of these two numerical descriptions does not require us to ignore the other considerable evidence that the number 144,000 is symbolic.

The biblical hope does not assign the redeemed to three different heavenly kingdoms or divide them into earthly and heavenly classes. There is "one body" that has "one hope" (Eph. 4:4). All believers in Christ have God as their Father and Jesus as their brother by virtue of the Spirit dwelling in them (Rom. 8:9–30;

THE APOSTLE PAUL

... one body and one Spirit ... one hope of your calling; one Lord, one faith, one baptism, one God and Father of all. (Eph. 4:4–6) cf. Gal. 3:27 – 4:7). A false view of Heaven leads to a false view of the church, and this in turn leads to a false view of the Christian life.[7]

Theologically, the most problematic aspect of the Jehovah's Witnesses' doctrine of the two classes of Christian believers is the notion that one class will live forever as spirits in Heaven while the other class will live forever (if they prove themselves worthy) as human beings on Earth. This flawed doctrine poses an important question, however: Just where will God's redeemed people live forever? And what will it be like? This is the subject of our final chapter.

SENSE

All of Christ's followers have the same faith and the same hope.

NONSENSE

The redeemed will be forever separated into different realms.

Chapter 17

WHEN HEAVEN AND EARTH SHALL BE ONE

God is going to live with us in a new heaven
and new earth.

One facet of the human condition is our apparent proclivity to extremism. The pendulum doesn't just swing from one side to the other; we *push* it, back and forth. Unfortunately, the solution to extremism is not necessarily splitting the difference or finding a position of moderation. Sometimes, moderation is just a euphemism for compromise.

Theology has its share of both extremism and compromise, including matters pertaining to Heaven and Hell. We have already seen some examples. Either the human soul is innately immortal and indestructible *or* it ceases to exist when the body dies. Either Hell is a physical place of endless, literal fire — perhaps some sort of star — *or* a metaphor for annihilation. Either the masses of unevangelized people throughout human history are all going to Hell *or* the vast majority of them will somehow be saved after all.

The truth cannot be discovered merely by looking for a mediating position. The soul *will* exist forever, but if condemned its existence will not qualify as life. Hell will be *eternal* punishment (not, say, a very long period of chastisement and rehabilitation), and the fire, though metaphorical, represents a punishment no less fearful. *Most* unevangelized people are apparently headed for Hell (as are those who *have* heard the gospel and rejected it), yet there will likely be billions of human beings outside the church whom God will save (notably those who die in the womb or in infancy), and God may find ways to save people we think cannot be reached.

Extremism and compromise with regard to Heaven manifest themselves in various specific issues, but the one to which we will give our attention in this concluding chapter is the question of the relationship of Heaven to Earth. There was a time when one could confidently speak of *the* traditional or popular view in Western culture: Earth is the training ground, the warm-up, for Heaven, our intended home; when people die, they go straight to Heaven or straight to Hell; Heaven is more or less everything Earth is not—an ethereal realm of spirits at eternal rest, or else a choir that sings incessantly for all time.

This is a view that is today parodied as much as it is preached. As we saw in chapter 1, the contemporary situation is that of a confusing array of diverse opinions. The various beliefs can be charted across two axes: the extremes of a theocentric and anthropocentric Heaven, and the extremes of a purely physical and a purely spiritual Heaven. Both sets of alternatives, we think, reflect confusion about the relationship of Heaven to Earth.

From Earth to Heaven and Back Again

The eternal home for God's people will not be this Earth alone, nor will it be Heaven alone; nor will some people go to Heaven while others live on the Earth. It will be what the Bible calls a "new heavens and new earth" (Isa. 65:17; 66:22; 2 Pet. 3:13; Rev. 21:1). The phrase "the heavens and the earth" in biblical usage usually (perhaps always) refers to the entirety of the physical universe (Gen. 1:1). The idea, then, is that we will live in a new universe.

What confuses many people on this issue is how the idea of a future new universe relates to the idea that we go to Heaven when we die. It turns out that *both* are true. When we die—if we are Christians—we go to be with Christ (2 Cor. 5:1–8; Phil. 1:21–23; cf. Luke 23:43). Since Christ is in Heaven, evidently believers go to Heaven when they die. However, this is not their "final destination."

When believers are in Heaven following their death, they do not have physical bodies (2 Cor. 5:6–8) but they await their resurrection at the end of history (1 Cor. 15:51–52; 1 Thess. 4:13–17).

A recent book by Randy Alcorn on Heaven proposes a different view of the matter. According to Alcorn, it is possible that humans during the intermediate state will possess "intermediate bodies," that is, bodies that are not completely glorified but allow us to be whole people while awaiting our final glory. He interprets what he calls the "heavenly dwelling" of 2 Corinthians 5:1–4 in this way.[1] This simply cannot be correct. Paul says,

> For we know that if our earthly house, a tent, is destroyed, we have a building from God, a house not made with hands, eternal in the heavens. And, in fact, we groan in this one, longing to put on our house from heaven, since, when we are clothed, we will not be found naked. Indeed, we who are in this tent groan, burdened as we are, because we do not want to be unclothed but clothed, so that mortality may be swallowed up by life. (2 Cor. 5:1–4 HCSB)

Whatever this "dwelling from heaven" (Alcorn's expression "heavenly dwelling" is a paraphrase) turns out to be and whenever it is actually acquired, Paul explicitly describes it as *"eternal* in the heavens." It cannot be both eternal and intermediate.

The idea that Paul is expressing here is that God has planned for us an eternal body that has a heavenly origin and will be immortal. That is our ultimate hope and future. The idea of living without a body did not appeal to Paul and is not a natural state for human beings. Yet "while we are at home in the body we are away from the Lord," and being with the Lord is what we want most. So, Paul says, we "would rather be away from the body and at home with the Lord" (2 Cor. 5:6–8). That situation will also be temporary; the implication of what Paul has said is that at the end of history we will be resurrected from the dead, and then we will be at home in the body—our new, eternal, immortal body—*and* with the Lord.

The biblical doctrine is not the view popular in Western culture, which is a view like this:

Mortal life ◀ Immortal bodiless life in Heaven

Nor is it this view, taught by Adventists and Jehovah's Witnesses:

Mortal life ◀ Nonexistence ◀ Resurrection to immortal bodily life

Nor is it the view suggested by Alcorn (though it is much closer):

Mortal life ◀ Bodily life in Heaven ◀ Resurrection to immortal bodily life

Rather, the biblical view is as follows:

Mortal life ◀ Bodiless life in Heaven ◀ Resurrection to immortal bodily life

Some people wonder why anyone who is already living with the Lord in Heaven would want or need to be resurrected from the dead. The answer is that we were not meant to live in a disembodied state in a purely spiritual Heaven. God created human beings to live as embodied beings on Earth. Our spiritual, intermediate state of rest in Heaven will be better than our troubled mortal life now, but it will not be nearly as wonderful as our resurrected, glorified embodied state on the future New Earth.

Jesus Christ's own history after becoming a human being sets the basic pattern in motion. He became a mortal man, died and rose again, ascended to Heaven, and will return bodily to Earth to establish his kingdom:

Jesus is raised
and goes to Heaven

Jesus lives as a
mortal man on Earth

Jesus returns
to Earth

The difference is that believers, unlike Jesus Christ, do not go to Heaven in their exalted, resurrected state. As Paul says, "the dead in Christ will rise first" when the Lord descends from Heaven, and then those who are alive on the Earth when the Lord comes "will be caught up together with them" (1 Thess. 4:16–17 NASB).[2] The resurrection, then, comes at the end of the age for believers. Christ has already risen from the dead as "the first fruits" of the resurrection. "Then at his coming those who belong to Christ" will be raised from the dead (1 Cor. 15:23).[3]

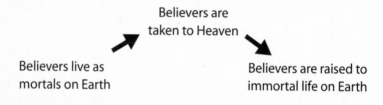

Believers are
taken to Heaven

Believers live as
mortals on Earth

Believers are raised to
immortal life on Earth

Rereading Revelation

Alcorn—whose book is in many respects commendable—takes a doggedly literalistic approach to many biblical texts about Heaven, especially those in Revelation. For example, he argues that the dead have bodies even while they await the resurrection because they "are described as wearing clothes" (Rev. 6:9–11).[4] But if we are to take the clothing literally, shall we also take literally the description of the dead in the very same text as positioned "under the altar" (v. 9)? Most interpreters rightly understand that Jesus does not have a literal sword coming out of his mouth (1:16), that Jesus will not literally spit "lukewarm" people out of his mouth (3:16), and that Jesus is not a lamb with seven horns and seven eyes (5:6). Alcorn, while he acknowledges that these statements should not be taken literally, proposes that statements in the book are to be taken literally unless doing so would "contradict known facts":

> When Jesus is described as a lamb with seven eyes, it contradicts known facts to take that literally. But would it contradict known facts to believe that on the New Earth there will be a great city with streets of gold and gates made of pearls (Revelation 21:21), and with trees and a river (22:1–2)?[5]

The problem with this approach of taking everything literally unless "it contradicts known facts" is that it encourages speculation in the wrong direction. Interpreters who approach Revelation in this way try to come up with literal explanations of symbolic language that was not intended literally, and the results are often fanciful.

Such excessive literalism also fails to consider the use of symbolic imagery throughout the book. For example, suppose we accept Alcorn's suggestion that the white robes given to the martyrs in Revelation 6:11 are literal clothes. In the next chapter the saints who came out of the Great Tribulation are described as wearing white robes, and "they have washed their robes and made them white in the blood of the Lamb" (7:9, 13–14). There seems to be no sensible way to take the white robes literally but not the washing of the robes in the Lamb's blood. Therefore, even though taking this picture literally contradicts no known facts, the best interpretation by far is to understand the white robes as nonliteral, symbolic elements of John's vision.

It is the genre of Revelation as a book of visions that ought to control our approach to its imagery. It is the book's genre, confirmed by evidence of apocalyptic symbolism throughout the book, as well as the heavenly setting of the visions, that leads interpreters to understand the clothing of the souls under the altar to be a nonliteral, symbolic picture.

A sounder approach to Revelation[6] has been proposed by New Testament scholar Vern S. Poythress. He distinguishes four "levels of communication" in the book's visions. These are not four different meanings (as in the older allegorical approach to the Bible) but four facets of the way meaning is conveyed in these passages. Put in simple terms, these four levels are the words John uses in the passage, what John sees in his vision, the persons or objects or events to which specific elements in the vision refer, and the symbolic significance of the imagery in the vision. Poythress calls these the linguistic, visionary, referential, and symbolical levels,[7] but we can think of them more simply as the word, vision, object, and symbolism levels.

An easy example is found in Revelation 5:6, where John says that he "saw ... a Lamb standing, as if slain, having seven horns and seven eyes, which are the seven Spirits of God, sent out into all the earth" (NASB). John here uses various *words*, including "lamb," "slain," "horns," and "eyes" to convey his message. These words build up a description of John's very bizarre *vision* (a lamb with seven horns and seven eyes!). The *object* represented in the vision by the "lamb" refers to Jesus Christ, who died on the cross, rose from the dead, and sent the Holy Spirit. The imagery reminds the readers of the Old Testament practice of sacrificing a lamb and the description of the Suffering Servant as having died "like a lamb that is led to the slaughter" (Isa. 53:7). The description therefore *symbolizes* the sacrificial death and resurrection of Christ. The horns and eyes are also symbolic of the exalted Christ's great power and knowledge.

The City on the Edge of Forever

We suggest that this approach of distinguishing what John *sees* in his visions from what those visions symbolically *represent* is helpful in understanding the climactic visions in Revelation about the New Jerusalem and the New Heaven and New Earth. Many evangelical Christians argue that the book's description of the New Jerusalem should be interpreted literally to refer to an actual physical city. Some evangelicals go so far as to argue that if we don't take the language of the New Jerusalem literally, we compromise the reliability of the Bible.

William R. Newell, writing in the 1930s, fretted: "If gold does not mean gold, nor pearls — pearls, nor precious stones — stones, nor exact measurements — real dimensions, then the Bible gives nothing accurate or reliable."[8] Randy Alcorn argues that the repeated use of the word "city" in Revelation 21 – 22 and the passage's detailed description "suggest that the term city isn't merely a figure of speech but a literal geographical location."[9] According to him, denying that the streets of gold and other physical descriptions, such as the city's dimensions, should be taken literally puts one on a slippery slope toward denying the resurrection hope:

If we assume the city's dimensions can't be real, people will likely believe the city isn't real. If it doesn't have its stated dimensions, then it's a short step to believing it doesn't have any dimensions at all. Then we think of the New Earth as not being a resurrected realm suited for resurrected people.[10]

These slippery-slope concerns are overblown. It is entirely possible to affirm the material reality of the New Earth as a realm for resurrected human beings while denying that the description of the New Jerusalem is meant to be taken literally. The key issue here is the *identification* of the New Jerusalem. John says that he saw the New Jerusalem "coming down out of heaven from God, prepared as a bride adorned for her husband" (Rev. 21:2). In verse 9 an angel tells John, "Come, I will show you the bride, the wife of the Lamb." As was just mentioned, the Lamb is Jesus Christ (5:6); and as most of us probably also know, the church (or, as Revelation puts it, "the saints") is the bride or wife of the Lamb (19:7–8; cf. 2 Cor. 11:2; Eph. 5:25–27). Therefore, the New Jerusalem is a symbol for the redeemed in their future glory, not a description of a literal location.[11]

Its description as a cube city made of transparent gold, with twelve large pearl gates guarded by twelve angels, with twelve foundation stones composed of twelve different kinds of precious stone, measuring 12,000 stadia in each direction, with walls 144 (i.e., 12 x 12) cubits high (Rev. 21:10–21), is symbolic of the church's role as a kind of spiritual Israel (note v. 12) and its being established in the teachings of the twelve apostles (v. 14). Just as we do not take Revelation's picture of Jesus as a lamb with seven horns and seven eyes as a description of Jesus' literal appearance, so we should not take literally the same book's picture of the redeemed in glory as a cube city measuring some 1,400 miles high that will descend from the sky and

C. S. LEWIS

All the scriptural imagery (harps, crowns, gold, etc.) is, of course, a merely symbolical attempt to express the inexpressible.... People who take these symbols literally might as well think that when Christ told us to be like doves, He meant that we were to lay eggs.[12]

land on the earth. The city coming down out of Heaven (21:2, 10) represents the fact that the redeemed people of God have their life from God; indeed, at the end of this age nearly all of the redeemed will be waiting in Heaven for their resurrection and glorification.

Making All Things New

Again, we are not denying that the future home of the redeemed will be a New Earth. Indeed, we insist on it. On this point, Alcorn is right: the hope of God's people is not an ethereal Heaven but a new universe in which redeemed human beings will live.

In what sense will the New Heavens and New Earth be "new"? On this question, commentators and theologians have generally debated two options. Some have argued for a "renewal" model, in which this universe is renewed, restored, or perfected. According to this renewal model, the New Heavens and New Earth will be this present universe purified of all evil, sin, suffering, and death. The opposing view is a "replacement" view, in which this universe is annihilated and replaced with a brand new, second universe created *ex nihilo* ("out of nothing").[13]

Both of these positions claim biblical support. Those who advocate the *renewal model* typically offer the following three arguments. (1) The word for "new" here (*kainos*) connotes newness in quality or nature, as compared to the Greek words *neos* and *neōteros*, which connote newness in time or origin. This linguistic argument does not seem strong enough to support the conclusion (e.g., in Rev. 2:17 the "new [*kainon*] name" is both new in origin and new in nature). And the "new [*kainēn*] Jerusalem" (21:2) cannot be the earthly city of Jerusalem transformed, can it? It seems better to let context determine the significance of *kainos*.

(2) In the immediate context, God says, "I am making all things new" (21:5), which would seem to be a clear affirmation of renewal, not replacement. This is a much stronger argument, though again, the immediate context also speaks of the "new Jerusalem" (v. 2).

(3) The Old Testament background favors understanding the newness as restoration (e.g., Isa. 65:18–25; Ezek. 28:25–26; 34:25–30).[14]

In favor of the *replacement model*, again three points may be highlighted. (1) Revelation 21:1 says that there will be no more sea, which implies a very different universe from the one in which we currently live. However, this is John's visionary experience, and it is clearly symbolic of there not being any more source of evil (cf. Dan. 7:3; Rev. 13:1, 6–7). We should therefore be wary of drawing any inferences from John's statement as to the actual form of the New Earth.

(2) The statements that "the first heaven and the first earth had passed away" and that "the first things have passed away" (21:1, 4) indicate an annihilation of the first heavens and earth and suggest that the new heavens and earth will be a *second* universe. However, this language was familiar to New Testament Christians from Isaiah and elsewhere as apocalyptic descriptions of the radical restoration to come. Paul can even describe Christians *now* as part of such a "new creation" in which "everything old has passed away" (2 Cor. 5:17).

(3) Elsewhere, Peter states that the present heavens and earth will be destroyed by fire and its very elements destroyed (2 Pet. 3:10–13). This is probably the strongest argument for the replacement view (even though this language has also been characterized as "apocalyptic").

We cannot help but notice that a similar debate has taken place with regard to the resurrection from the dead. Will resurrection mean a renewal of the body (reanimation and perfection) or a creation of a second body (replacement)? In the case of Jesus himself, his dead body was brought back to life (reanimated) and glorified as an immortal, incorruptible body. Believers look forward to having the same kind of body (see ch. 8). However, for nearly all believers, resurrection will not mean the reanimation of an actually existing corpse, because most of their bodies will long since have disintegrated into dust.

BEN WITHERINGTON III

The final state is represented as transpiring not when believers go up to heaven but when God and heaven come down permanently.[15]

But this won't be a problem for God! He will be able to create a new body for those believers—one that will truly be them, yet gloriously new as well. (We may assume that in the case of believers whose dead bodies are still intact at the resurrection, those bodies will be reanimated in the same way as Jesus' body was.) Those believers who are still alive when Christ returns to raise the dead will be changed or transformed, with immortality and incorruption put on their existing bodies (1 Cor. 15:51–54). To put it another way: in the resurrection, *some bodies will be "renewed" and other bodies will be "replaced," but the end result for both will be the same.* All of the redeemed will have perfect, glorified, immortal, incorruptible, spiritually empowered human bodies, capable of living in God's eternal, heavenly kingdom in the New Heavens and New Earth.

We suggest that looking at the resurrection in this way helps us to move past the renewal/replacement debate with regards to the New Heavens and New Earth. If we adopt a renewal model, we must still recognize that the new universe will not be simply a cleaned-up version of this one, but will be a world transformed, fit for immortal beings. If we adopt a replacement model, we must still recognize that the new universe will have important similarities to this one, because it will be a world for human beings. Perhaps we may speak of the universe itself as destined for resurrection.[16] The world itself will "pass away" (Matt. 24:35) in order to be made anew as a fitting eternal habitat for a resurrected humanity.

Thinking of the eternal state of the blessed as a resurrected New Heavens and New Earth also provides a way to resolve the debate between those who advocate a "theocentric" view of Heaven as eternal contemplation of the divine glory (what is called the "beatific vision") and those who favor an "anthropocentric" view of Heaven as an unending paradise of human activity (see ch. 1). Resurrection for Jesus Christ meant both return to human life (with the capacity for interaction with other people and such mundane activities as eating) and exaltation to the immediate presence of God. It will mean that for us, too.

The extremes of a purely God-centered view of Heaven as endless contemplation of the Divine and a purely man-centered view of Heaven as an unending theme park adventure with our earthly family and friends must both be rejected. In its place we must develop a Christ-centered view of eternal life in the New Heavens and New Earth, in which God dwells with the redeemed human race, in which a new extended divine "family" of God enjoys God and each other forever. Jesus promised that his followers would "inherit the earth" *and* "see God" (Matt. 5:5, 8), and so they shall when God comes down to live with us forever on the New Earth. The Head of this "family" will be Jesus Christ, the incarnate Son; included under his headship will be both angelic "sons of God" and human "sons of God." We call this Christ-centered way of looking at eternal life an Incarnational model.

God-Centered Model	Man-Centered Model	Christ-Centered Model
Heaven only	Earth only, or Earth-like Heaven only	New Heavens and New Earth
Beatific vision	Unlimited human pleasures	Extended "family" of God
Resurrection as exaltation of the soul to immortality	Resurrection as resuscitation of the body	Resurrection as glorification of the whole human person, body and soul
Dissolution of all human relationships	Restoration of all human relationships	Transformation of all human relationships

This Christ-centered view of eternity is gloriously expressed in John's climactic vision:

> And I heard a loud voice from the throne saying, "Behold, the dwelling place of God is with man. He will dwell with them, and they will be his people, and God himself will be with them as their God. He will wipe away every tear from their eyes, and death shall be no more, neither shall there be mourning nor crying nor pain anymore, for the former things have passed away."

And he who was seated on the throne said, "Behold, I am making all things new." Also he said, "Write this down, for these words are trustworthy and true." And he said to me, "It is done! I am the Alpha and the Omega, the beginning and the end. To the thirsty I will give from the spring of the water of life without payment. The one who conquers will have this heritage, and I will be his God and he will be my son." (Rev. 21:3–7 ESV)

SENSE

We will live forever in a new universe, fit for immortal beings.

NONSENSE

The book of Revelation literally describes that new universe.

RECOMMENDED READING

Most people do not need to read dozens of books on the subjects of Heaven and Hell. However, if this book has whetted your appetite for more, here are ten books that we think are especially worthy of your time.

Cooper, John W. *Body, Soul, and Life Everlasting: Biblical Anthropology and the Monism-Dualism Debate*. Grand Rapids: Eerdmans, 1989. Advanced study of the issue of the body-soul issue, which also discusses the soul's existence after death.

Cullmann, Oscar. *Immortality of the Soul or Resurrection from the Dead? The Witness of the New Testament*. London: Epworth, 1958. This older, short book, available online at *www.religion-online.org/showbook.asp?title=1115*, explains why resurrection is central to the biblical view of the afterlife.

Fudge, Edward William, and Robert A. Peterson. *Two Views of Hell: A Biblical and Theological Dialogue*. Downers Grove, IL: InterVarsity Press, 2000. Articulate defenders of annihilationism and the traditional view of Hell square off.

Hoekema, Anthony A. *The Bible and the Future*. Grand Rapids: Eerdmans, 1979. Excellent textbook on eschatology (the study of last things), with especially good and relevant chapters on immortality, the intermediate state, resurrection, the final judgment, eternal punishment, and the new earth.

Martindale, Wayne. *Beyond the Shadowlands: C. S. Lewis on Heaven and Hell*. Wheaton, IL: Crossway, 2005. A delightful study of Lewis's views that also effectively introduces the reader to several of his lesser-known, valuable writings.

McGrath, Alister E. *A Brief History of Heaven*. Oxford, UK: Blackwell, 2003. An elegant history of (mostly Christian) beliefs about Heaven.

Milne, Bruce. *The Message of Heaven and Hell*. The Bible Speaks Today, series ed. Derek Tidball. Downers Grove, IL: InterVarsity Press, 2002. Solid exposition of key passages in the Old and New Testaments.

Morgan, Christopher W., and Robert A. Peterson, eds. *Hell under Fire: Modern Scholarship Reinvents Eternal Punishment*. Grand Rapids: Zondervan, 2004. Collection of essays, several of them excellent.

Okholm, Dennis L., and Timothy R. Phillips, eds. *Four Views on Salvation in a Pluralistic World*. Counterpoint Series, ed. Stanley N. Gundry. Grand Rapids: Zondervan, 1996. Presents the full range of views: that all religions can lead to God (John Hick), that Christ saves many outside of Christianity (Clark Pinnock), that Christ might save some outside of Christianity (Alister McGrath), and that "except perhaps in very special circumstances" only those who explicitly believe in Christ will be saved (Douglas Geivett and Gary Phillips).

Tiessen, Terrance L. *Who Can Be Saved? Reassessing Salvation in Christ and World Religions*. Downers Grove, IL: InterVarsity Press, 2004. Although we don't agree with Tiessen's view, this book is an interesting, informative study of the questions regarding salvation outside the Christian church.

NOTES

Chapter 1: The Make-Your-Own-Heaven Game

1. We discuss the evidence for God in *20 Compelling Evidences That God Exists* (Colorado Springs, CO: Cook, 2001).
2. Blaise Pascal, *Pensées*, trans. W. F. Trotter (many editions), no. 194.
3. Emanuel Swedenborg, *Heaven and Its Wonders, and Hell: From Things Heard and Seen* (New York: Swedenborg Foundation, 1952), preface; online at *http://swedenborg.newearth.org/hh/hh01.html#Swedenborg's %20Preface*.
4. Betty J. Eadie, *Embraced by the Light* (New York: Bantam, 1994).
5. Mary Baker Eddy, *Science and Health, with Key to the Scriptures* (Boston: Writings of Mary Baker Eddy, 1910; many editions), 587, 291, respectively.
6. Anthony DeStefano, *A Travel Guide to Heaven* (New York: Doubleday, 2003), 3.
7. For a scientific and Christian critique of general UFO beliefs, see Hugh Ross, Kenneth R. Samples, and Mark Clark, *Lights in the Sky and Little Green Men: A Rational Christian Look at UFOs and Extraterrestrials* (Colorado Springs, CO: NavPress, 2002).
8. Colleen McDannell and Bernhard Lang, *Heaven: A History*, 2d ed. (New Haven, CT: Yale Univ. Press, 2001), xiii–xiv, xviii (quoted).
9. Ibid., 178–80.
10. Ibid., 180.
11. John Wesley, *Works* (Nashville: Abingdon, 1985), 1:104–105, quoted in Jerry L. Walls, *Heaven: The Logic of Eternal Joy* (Oxford: Oxford Univ. Press, 2002), 5.

Chapter 2: The First Person You Meet in Heaven

1. The same point is made, though developed in another way, by Adrio König, *The Eclipse of Christ in Eschatology: Toward a Christ-Centered Approach* (Grand Rapids: Eerdmans; London: Marshall, Morgan & Scott, 1989).
2. Our translation from the Greek. The traditional English translation has "men" and "man" instead of "human beings" and "human," although the latter are more correct in this context.

3. Kenneth D. Boa and Robert M. Bowman Jr., *Sense and Nonsense about Angels and Demons* (Grand Rapids: Zondervan, 2007), ch. 8.

4. The Greek word *mōre* (usually translated "fool!"), from which we derive "moron," was a term of abuse meaning a complete fool or idiot.

5. The word translated "hell" in these passages is *Gehenna*; see chapter 4.

6. We discuss this question in chapter 15.

7. See Boa and Bowman, *Sense and Nonsense about Angels and Demons*, ch. 21.

Chapter 3: Speaking of Heavens and Hells

1. Translation ours.

2. On the doctrine that angels are incorporeal, see Boa and Bowman, *Sense and Nonsense about Angels and Demons*, ch. 6.

3. Mortimer J. Adler, *The Angels and Us* (New York: Macmillan, 1982), 37.

4. Homer, *The Odyssey* 11.487, as quoted in Peter G. Bolt, "Life, Death, and the Afterlife in the Greco-Roman World," in *Life in the Face of Death: The Resurrection Message of the New Testament*, ed. Richard N. Longenecker (Grand Rapids: Eerdmans, 1998), 63.

5. Samuele Bacchiocchi, *Immortality or Resurrection? A Biblical Study on Human Nature and Destiny* (Berrien Springs, MI: Biblical Perspectives, 1997), 170. We give some attention to this book because Bacchiocchi is one of the most accomplished and sophisticated biblical scholars defending the Adventist position.

6. Some Christians argue that Luke 16:19 – 31 cannot be a parable because Jesus refers to some persons by name (Lazarus, Abraham), something he doesn't do in other parables. However, we know of no hermeneutical reason why the use of specific personal names would disqualify a story from being a parable. As a matter of literary analysis, the fact that this story begins in the exact same way as the preceding parable of the rich man's unrighteous manager (Luke 16:1 – 13) strongly supports identifying this story also as a parable: "There was a rich man" (*anthrōpos tis ēn plousios*, Luke 16:1, 19). These parables are the second and third of a series of parables about the misuse of wealth that begins with the parable of the prodigal son (Luke 15:11 – 32).

7. Bacchiocchi, *Immortality or Resurrection?* 172 – 76. He cites a work entitled *Discourse to the Greeks concerning Hades*, attributing it to the late first-century Jewish writer Josephus, as an example of contemporary Jewish belief in Hades and Abraham's bosom. However, this work was not written by Josephus; it was almost certainly written by Hippolytus, a Christian writer of the early third century.

8. Ibid., 171.

9. Bacchiocchi, *Immortality or Resurrection?* 172.

10. Philip S. Johnston, *Shades of Sheol: Death and Afterlife in the Old Testament* (Downers Grove, IL: InterVarsity Press, 2002), 74, citing R. Laird Harris, "The Meaning of the Word Sheol as Shown by Parallels in Poetic Texts," *BETS* 4 (1961): 129–35; "Why She'ol Was Translated 'Grave,'" in *The Making of a Contemporary Translation*, ed. Kenneth L. Barker (Grand Rapids: Zondervan, 1987), 75–92.

11. See Johnston, *Shades of Sheol*, 80–83.

12. Gary A. Lee, "Gehenna," in *The International Standard Bible Encyclopedia*, ed. Geoffrey W. Bromiley, rev. ed. (Grand Rapids: Eerdmans, 1982), 2:423.

13. Henri Blocher, "Everlasting Punishment and the Problem of Evil," in *Universalism and the Doctrine of Hell*, Papers presented at the Fourth Edinburgh Conference on Christian Dogmatics, 1991, ed. Nigel M. de S. Cameron (Carlisle, UK: Paternoster; Grand Rapids: Baker, 1992), 306 n. 89; Peter Head, "The Duration of Divine Judgment in the New Testament," in *Eschatology in the Bible and Theology: Evangelical Essays at the Dawn of a New Millennium*, ed. Kent E. Brower and Mark W. Elliott (Downers Grove, IL: InterVarsity Press, 1997), 223. The point has been acknowledged by one opponent of the traditional view of Hell: William Edward Fudge, *The Fire That Consumes: A Biblical and Historical Study of Final Punishment* (Houston: Providential, 1982), 161.

Chapter 4: Till Death Do Us Part

1. Johnston, *Shades of Sheol*, 33–34.

2. Bacchiocchi, *Immortality or Resurrection?* 39.

3. "Ecclesiastes," in *Insight on the Scriptures* (Brooklyn: Watchtower Bible & Tract Society, 1988), 1:675.

Chapter 5: Soul Man

1. Oscar Cullmann, *Immortality of the Soul or Resurrection from the Dead? The Witness of the New Testament* (London: Epworth, 1958); all citations from the online edition at *www.religion-online.org/showbook. asp?title=1115*.

2. See Bacchiocchi, *Immortality or Resurrection?* 21.

3. E.g., "Inherent Immortality or Resurrection—Which?" *Watchtower* (April 1, 1982), 15–16; "The Truth about Hell," *Watchtower* (Oct. 1, 1989), 7; "How Strong Is Your Belief in the Resurrection?" *Watchtower* (July 1, 1998), 9, 12.

4. In Greek, *sarkos anastasin*; in Latin, *carnis resurrectionem*. The traditional English translation, "the resurrection of the body," is not so

much inaccurate as less explicit than the ancient forms. Cullmann, in ch. 3 of *Immortality of the Soul or Resurrection from the Dead?* considers the creed to be in "error" in its use of *flesh* because for Paul the flesh was "the power of death, which must be destroyed." But there is no reason why the creed should be expected to use the word "flesh" in this specialized Pauline sense, since the biblical writers use the word in different ways (see, e.g., John 1:14; Acts 2:26, 31).

5. Cullmann, conclusion of *Immortality of the Soul or Resurrection from the Dead?*

6. Oddly, the NASB renders *nephesh* as "soul" in verse 4 but "person" in verse 20. (The NRSV uses "person" in both verses.) All quotes from Ezekiel 18 are from the NASB.

7. See their *Reasoning from the Scriptures* (Brooklyn: Watchtower Bible & Tract Society, 1985), 174.

8. Cullmann, ch. 2 of *Immortality of the Soul or Resurrection from the Dead?*

Chapter 6: Between Death and Glory

1. Bruce M. Metzger, *A Textual Commentary on the Greek New Testament* (New York: United Bible Societies, 1971, corrected edition 1975), 223 (commenting on John 8:25). The same point is made by Joseph Hong, "Understanding and Translating 'Today' in Luke 23:43," *BT* 46 (1995): 411. Greg Stafford, a Jehovah's Witness, appeals to a point located between *sēmeron* ("today") and *met'* ("with") in a fourth-century manuscript called the Codex Vaticanus as evidence of early punctuation of the text placing a break after "today." See Greg Stafford, *Jehovah's Witnesses Defended: An Answer to Scholars and Critics*, 2d ed. (Huntington Beach, CA: Elihu, 2000), 546–47. However, to our knowledge no other ancient manuscript has this same lower point, which may have been either an accidental stray dot or a point inserted by a later copyist that reflected only his opinion.

2. Klyne R. Snodgrass, "Amen," in *Baker Encyclopedia of the Bible*, ed. Walter A. Elwell (Grand Rapids: Baker, 1988), 1:69.

3. Matt. 5:18, 26; 6:2, 5, 16; 8:10; 10:15, 23, 42; 11:11; 13:17; 16:28; 17:20; 18:3, 13, 18, 19 [some manuscripts omit *amēn*]; 19:23, 28; 21:21, 31; 23:36; 24:2, 34, 47; 25:12, 40, 45; 26:13, 21, 34; Mark 3:28; 8:12; 9:1, 41; 10:15, 29; 11:23; 12:43; 13:30; 14:9, 18, 25, 30; Luke 4:24; 12:37; 18:17, 29; 21:32; 23:43; John 1:51; 3:3, 5, 11; 5:19, 24, 25; 6:26, 32, 47, 53; 8:34, 51, 58; 10:1, 7; 12:24; 13:16, 20, 21, 38; 14:12; 16:20, 23; 21:18. This list includes sayings using the plural for "you" (*hymin*, 66 times) and the singular for "you" (*soi*, 9 times).

4. The only qualification to this point is that in about thirty-one of the seventy-five occurrences of the formula "Amen I say to you," the connective *hoti* ("that") is used to connect the formula to the statement that follows.

5. E. W. Bullinger, *How to Enjoy the Bible*, 5th ed. (London: Eyre & Spottiswoode, 1921), 48, cited in Stafford, *Jehovah's Witnesses Defended*, 550; see also Bullinger's note in *The Companion Bible* (London: Oxford Univ. Press, 1932), Appendix 173.

6. Revelation 2:7 promises that those who "overcome" will be allowed "to eat of the tree of life which is in the Paradise of God" (NASB). Although this statement could refer to a heavenly Paradise, more likely it looks forward to the new heavens and new earth and the new Jerusalem, where the "tree of life" will be (21:1–3, 10–11; 22:1–2). We discuss these passages later.

7. Perhaps the first to critique the NWT on Philippians 1:21–24 was Walter Martin; see his *The Kingdom of the Cults*, rev. and updated ed., Ravi Zacharias, gen. ed. (Minneapolis: Bethany, 2003), 97–99.

8. The only other version that comes close is the *Emphatic Diaglott*, a nineteenth-century unorthodox version that was a favorite of the Jehovah's Witnesses before they produced their own version.

9. "Appendix 5D: The Releasing to Be with Christ," in *The New World Translation: With References* (Brooklyn: Watchtower Bible & Tract Society, 1984), 1578; "A Theological Dilemma," *Watchtower* (March 1, 1995), 30.

10. The word *analysai* is used in the Apocrypha literally to mean both "return" (2 Macc. 15:28; Wisd. 2:1) and "depart" (Judith 13:1; 3 Macc. 5:44).

11. Cullmann, *Immortality of the Soul or Resurrection from the Dead?* ch. 4; online at *www.religion-online.org/showchapter.asp?title=1115&C=1218.*

Chapter 7: Touch Me and See

1. We discuss the basic factual evidence for the resurrection in *20 Compelling Evidences That God Exists*, chs. 15–17.

2. See the *Qurʾan*, Sura 4:157–58.

3. Mary Baker Eddy, *Science and Health*, 44.

4. Gloria and Kenneth Wapnick, *The Most Commonly Asked Questions about A Course in Miracles*, Q. 23 (online at *www.miraclestudies.net/Question23.html*).

5. Sun Myung Moon, *Divine Principle* (Washington, D.C.: Holy Spirit Association for the Unification of World Christianity, 1977), 360.

6. Robert M. Bowman Jr., *Jehovah's Witnesses* (Zondervan Guide to Cults & Religious Movements; Grand Rapids: Zondervan, 1995), 39–70.

7. For a skeptical use of this theory, see Richard C. Carrier, "The Spiritual Body of Christ and the Legend of the Empty Tomb," in *The Empty Tomb: Jesus beyond the Grave*, ed. Robert M. Price and Jeffery Jay Lowder (Amherst, NY: Prometheus, 2005), 105–231.

8. McDannell and Lang, *Heaven: A History*, 35.

9. For our purposes, we need not concern ourselves with the alleged discrepancies among the Gospel resurrection accounts, which do not amount to anything of significance with regard to the nature of the resurrection.

10. We are here assuming, following nearly all biblical scholars, that Mark 16:9–20 (the "Long Ending of Mark") was not part of the original Gospel.

11. "How Does Christ Return?" *Watchtower* (June 15, 1982), 17.

12. *Reasoning from the Scriptures*, 335.

13. Ibid.

14. The reasons are twofold: (1) the passage is missing from the earliest Greek manuscripts, and later manuscripts have a variety of endings, not just the one familiar from the King James Version; and (2) the passage has tell-tale internal signs of having been added by a later hand (e.g., Mark 16:9 introduces Mary Magdalene as if she had not just been mentioned twice, Mark 15:47–16:1). Almost any commentary on Mark will provide the details. This fact about the ending of Mark is now conceded in the Jehovah's Witnesses' publications: *Insight on the Scriptures* (Brooklyn: Watchtower Bible and Tract Society, 1988), 2:338; "Snake Handling in Worship—Is that What God Approves?" *Awake!* (August 8, 1973), 5–7.

15. Daniel B. Wallace, *Greek Grammar beyond the Basics: An Exegetical Syntax of the New Testament* (Grand Rapids: Zondervan, 1996), 437–38.

Chapter 8: O Death, Where Is Your Sting?

1. See chapter 8 and notes 68–71.

2. Augustine, *Questions* 66.7 (*Fathers of the Church* 70.148), as quoted in Gerald Bray, *Romans* (ACCS; Downers Grove, IL: InterVarsity Press, 1998), 6:213.

3. See Robert M. Bowman Jr., "Romans 8:11 and the Resurrection Body," online *www.biblicalapologetics.net/NTVerse/Romans8_11_Resurrection_Body.htm*.

4. The last commentator of any note to espouse this view of Romans 8:11 was apparently a German commentator of the 1930s named H.

Leitzmann; see James D. G. Dunn, *Romans 1–8* (WBC 38A; Dallas: Word, 1988), 432.

5. Douglas Moo, *The Epistle to the Romans* (NICNT; Grand Rapids: Eerdmans, 1996), 493.

6. The Jehovah's Witnesses' version of the Bible, the New World Translation, renders Romans 8:23 "the release from our bodies by ransom." The phrase here is *tēn apolutrōsin tou sōmatos hēmōn* (lit., "the redemption of our body"). Lexically, *apolutrōsis* followed by the genitive could mean either "redemption from" (in biblical usage, only in Heb. 9:15) or "redemption of" (e.g., Eph. 1:14); context must determine which it is. That "redemption of" is meant here is evident from the context, as we have explained.

7. Jehovah's Witnesses throughout their publications appeal to 1 Corinthians 15:45, 50, in support of their belief in a nonphysical resurrection. Skeptics often appeal to the same sort of interpretation of 1 Corinthians 15 to help debunk the resurrection of Jesus as historical fact: see, e.g., Carrier, "The Spiritual Body of Christ and the Legend of the Empty Tomb," 114–39.

8. Anthony C. Thiselton, *The First Epistle to the Corinthians: A Commentary on the Greek Text* (NIGTC; Grand Rapids: Eerdmans, 2000), 1192.

9. Ben Witherington III, *The Paul Quest: The Renewed Search for the Jew of Tarsus* (Downers Grove, IL: InterVarsity Press, 1998), 150–51.

10. Aeschylus, *Eumenides* 647–48 (frequently quoted as part of the background of Paul's teaching on resurrection).

Chapter 9: The Bad News Bears Repeating

1. See, e.g., the findings of the July 1998 Harris poll reported at *www.pollingreport.com/religion2.htm* (accessed 12/31/05).

2. For a longer list of views on what will happen to the unrighteous, see David J. Powys, "The Nineteenth and Twentieth Century Debate about Hell and Universalism," in *Universalism and the Doctrine of Hell*, ed. de S. Cameron (Carlisle, UK: Paternoster; Grand Rapids: Baker, 1992), 95, 132 n. 81, 137–38.

3. Pluralist universalism is associated especially with philosopher John Hick; see his contribution and the criticisms of his respondents in *Four Views on Salvation in a Pluralistic World*, ed. Dennis L. Okholm and Timothy R. Phillips (Grand Rapids: Zondervan, 1996).

4. See Morwenna Ludlow, "Universalism in the History of Christianity," in *Universal Salvation? The Current Debate*, ed. Robin A. Perry and Christopher H. Partridge (Grand Rapids: Eerdmans, 2004), 191–218. For an attempt to prove that universalism dominated early church

thought before Augustine, see J. W. Hanson, *Universalism: The Prevailing Doctrine of the Christian Church during Its First Five Hundred Years* (Boston: Universalist, 1899). Hanson appeals to silence (e.g., the early creeds don't mention eternal punishment), resorts to strained interpretations similar to those used by Universalists in regards to the Bible, and ignores some contrary evidence.

5. Clement of Alexandria (c. 150–215) seems not to have been a universalist, though he is sometimes cited as such. However, he may have paved the way for Origen to develop universalism (see Fudge, *The Fire That Consumes*, 340–42).

6. See Frederick W. Norris, "Universal Salvation in Origen and Maximus," in *Universalism and the Doctrine of Hell*, ed. de S. Cameron, 35–72.

7. Recent defenses of Christian universalism include David Lowes Watson, *God Does Not Foreclose: The Universal Promise of Salvation* (Nashville: Abingdon, 1990); Jan Bonda, *The One Purpose of God: An Answer to the Doctrine of Eternal Punishment* (Grand Rapids: Eerdmans, 1998); Thomas Talbott, *The Inescapable Love of God* (n.p.: Universal Publishers, 1999); Randy Klassen, *What Does the Bible Really Say about Hell? Wrestling with the Traditional View* (Living Issues Discussion Series 2; Telford, PA: Pandora; Scottdale, PA: Herald Press, 2001). See also Talbott's contributions to *Universal Salvation? The Current Debate*, ed. Perry and Partridge, cited earlier.

8. Douglas J. Moo, "Paul on Hell," in *Hell under Fire: Modern Scholarship Reinvents Eternal Punishment*, ed. Christopher W. Morgan and Robert A. Peterson (Grand Rapids: Zondervan, 2004), 99–100. The entire article is excellent and deserving of study.

9. For a contrary opinion by a renowned theologian, see B. B. Warfield, "Are They Few that Be Saved?" in *Biblical and Theological Studies* (1952), 334–50. If Jesus' statement contrasting the many who go down the path of destruction with the few that find life does not take into consideration those who die in infancy, the total number of people who are given eternal life might end up outnumbering those who don't (see ch. 15).

10. J. W. Hanson, *Bible Threatenings Explained* (Boston: Universalist, 1897), see *www.tentmaker.org/books/BibleThreateningsExplained.html*.

11. John Blanchard, *Whatever Happened to Hell?* (Darlington, Eng.: Evangelical Press, 1993), 204.

12. J. I. Packer, "Evangelicals and the Way of Salvation: New Challenges to the Gospel: Universalism, and Justification by Faith," in *Evangelical Affirmations*, ed. Kenneth S. Kantzer and Carl F. H. Henry (Grand Rapids: Zondervan, 1990), 114.

13. E.g., Lee Salisbury, "Eternity Explained," True Grace Ministries, n.d.; see *www.duc.auburn.edu/~allenkc/eternityexplained.html* (accessed 9/5/06). The argument is ubiquitous in Christian universalist literature.

14. Gen. 9:12, 16; 17:7, 8, 13, 19; 48:4; Ex. 12:14, 17; 27:21; 28:43; 29:28; 30:21; 31:16, 17; Lev. 6:18, 22; 7:34, 36; 10:9, 15; 16:29, 31, 34; 17:7; 23:21, 31, 41; 24:3, 8, 9; Num. 10:8; 15:15; 18:8, 11, 19, 23; 19:10, 21; 2 Sam. 23:5; 1 Chron. 16:17; Job 41:4; Ps. 105:10; Isa. 24:5; 55:3, 13; 61:8; Jer. 5:22; 50:5; Ezek. 16:20.

15. Job 3:18; 10:22; 22:15; Ps. 24:7, 9; Isa. 58:12; Jer. 6:16; 18:15, 16; Micah 2:9; Hab. 3:6; Jonah 2:6.

Chapter 10: Just Don't Go There!

1. Christopher W. Morgan, "Biblical Theology: Three Pictures of Hell," in *Hell under Fire*, ed. Morgan and Peterson, 142.

Chapter 11: Hell to Pay

1. For example, the Jehovah's Witnesses' New World Translation renders the word as "cutting-off" instead of "punishment" in Matt. 25:46.

2. Paul Helm, "Are They Few that Be Saved?" in *Universalism and the Doctrine of Hell*, ed. de S. Cameron, 258.

3. Richard Bauckham, *Jude, 2 Peter* (WBC 50; Waco, TX: Word, 1983), 53.

4. C. S. Lewis, *The Problem of Pain* (New York: Macmillan, 1944), 124.

5. The point has been frequently made, e.g., David G. Moore, *The Battle for Hell: A Survey and Evaluation of Evangelicals' Growing Attraction to the Doctrine of Annihilationism* (Lanham, MD: Univ. Press of America, 1995), 18–20 (although we differ with Moore's handling of some of the examples).

6. The NRSV has "destroyed" in two of these texts; cf. "ruined," ESV, NASB, NIV, NKJV.

Chapter 12: The Eternal Fire

1. Edward William Fudge, "Part One: The Case for Conditionalism," in *Two Views of Hell: A Biblical & Theological Dialogue*, by Edward William Fudge and Robert A. Peterson (Downers Grove, IL: InterVarsity Press, 2000), 28.

2. Ibid., 44, 71.

3. Grammatically, the words "of eternal fire" can modify either "example" or "punishment." If the former, the text would be saying, "they serve as an example of eternal fire by undergoing punishment"; if the latter, "they serve as an example by undergoing punishment of eternal

fire." Bauckham (*Jude, 2 Peter*, 55), like most biblical scholars, thinks the latter is "perhaps better."

4. Revelation 19:3 speaks of the smoke rising from the destruction of Babylon the Great, which, while not Hell, is part of the same complex of visions of the final disposition of the wicked.

5. Fudge, *The Fire That Consumes*, 428.

6. Fudge (ibid., 300), citing Harold E. Guillebaud, *The Righteous Judge: A Study of the Biblical Doctrine of Everlasting Punishment* (Taunton, UK: Phoenix, n.d.), 24. Bacchiocchi repeats the argument, using the same quotation from Guillebaud (without crediting Fudge), in *Immortality or Resurrection?* 213.

7. Fudge, *The Fire That Consumes*, 303–4; Bacchiocchi, *Immortality or Resurrection?* 214.

8. Fudge, *The Fire That Consumes*, 304.

9. David Powys, *"Hell": A Hard Look at a Hard Question: The Fate of the Unrighteous in New Testament Thought* (Paternoster Biblical and Theological Monographs; Carlisle, UK: Paternoster, 1998), 371–72.

10. G. K. Beale, *The Book of Revelation: A Commentary on the Greek Text* (NIGTC; Grand Rapids: Eerdmans, 1999), 1030.

11. Augustine of Hippo, *City of God* 20.22, 21.9, in *A Select Library of the Nicene and Post-Nicene Fathers of the Christian Church*, ed. Philip Schaff (Grand Rapids: Eerdmans reprint, n.d.), 2:443, 461; online at *www.ccel.org/ccel/schaff/npnf102.html*.

12. John of Damascus, *An Exposition of the Orthodox Faith* 4.27, from *A Select Library of the Nicene and Post-Nicene Fathers of the Christian Church*, series 2, ed. Alexander Roberts and James Donaldson, vol. 9 (Oak Harbor, WA: Logos Research Systems, 1997), online at *www.ccel. org/fathers2/NPNF2–09/Npnf2–09–31.htm*.

13. John Calvin, *Institutes of the Christian Religion*, 3.25.12, ed. John T. McNeill, trans. Ford Lewis Battles (LCC 20–21; Philadelphia: Westminster, 1960), 1007.

14. William G. T. Shedd, *Dogmatic Theology*, 3rd ed., ed. Alan W. Gomes (Phillipsburg, NJ: Presbyterian & Reformed, 2003), 892. Shedd is a nineteenth-century Calvinist theologian and author of a notable defense of the belief in Hell.

15. Gordon R. Lewis and Bruce A. Demarest, *Integrative Theology* (Grand Rapids: Zondervan, 1994), 3:470, 474.

16. Beale, *Book of Revelation*, 1029.

17. J. Dwight Pentecost, *Things to Come: A Study in Biblical Eschatology* (Grand Rapids: Zondervan, 1964), 560, 561, quoting C. T. Schwartze, "The Bible and Science on the Everlasting Fire," *BSac* 95 (1938): 105–12.

18. Henry M. Morris, *The Revelation Record: A Scientific and Devotional Commentary on the Book of Revelation* (Wheaton, IL: Tyndale; San Diego: Creation-Life, 1983), 431.
19. John Walvoord, "The Literal View," in *Four Views on Hell*, ed. William Crockett (Grand Rapids: Zondervan, 1992), 28.
20. Walvoord, "Response to William V. Crockett," in *Four Views on Hell*, 77–79.

Chapter 13: One Way, One Truth

1. We discuss the evidence for God and his redeeming revelation in Christ in *20 Compelling Evidences that God Exists*.
2. We are aware of the "New Perspective on Paul" that rejects this traditional evangelical understanding of Paul's teaching on works and justification. On this subject, see especially Stephen Westerholm, *Perspectives Old and New on Paul: The "Lutheran" Paul and His Critics* (Grand Rapids: Eerdmans, 2003), a thorough, academic study; see Mark Husbands and Daniel J. Treier, eds., *Justification: What's at Stake in the Current Debates* (Downers Grove, IL: InterVarsity Press, 2004), for a more popular-level introduction.
3. C. S. Lewis, "Man or Rabbit?" in *God in the Dock*, ed. Walter Hooper (Grand Rapids: Eerdmans, 1970), 109, quoted in Wayne Martindale, *Beyond the Shadowlands: C. S. Lewis on Heaven & Hell* (Wheaton, IL: Crossway, 2005), 44.
4. An interesting recent defense of this position is James R. Edwards, *Is Jesus the Only Savior?* (Grand Rapids: Eerdmans, 2005).
5. Terrance L. Tiessen, *Who Can Be Saved? Reassessing Salvation in Christ and World Religions* (Downers Grove, IL: InterVarsity Press, 2004), 126.
6. Ibid., 158.

Chapter 14: If I Should Die before I Hear

1. We are here ignoring *pluralism*, which denies that Jesus Christ is the only Savior, as well as *universalism*, which maintains that everyone will be saved (whether by Jesus Christ alone, as in Christian universalism, or by various means of salvation).
2. Theologians as diverse as Thomas Aquinas, Jacobus Arminius, and J. Oliver Buswell Jr. have supported some form of the premortem revelation view; see John Sanders, *No Other Name? An Investigation into the Destiny of the Unevangelized* (Grand Rapids: Eerdmans, 1992), 154–56. Tiessen (*Who Can Be Saved?* 116–19) also endorses the idea of premortem revelations to those with no human witness, although they do not seem essential to his view.

3. The nineteenth-century Catholic scholar John Henry Cardinal Newman is the best-known advocate of the final option view; see Sanders, *No Other Name?* 164–67. For a recent variation of this view, see Tiessen, *Who Can Be Saved?* 216–25. On Tiessen's view, everyone already has an opportunity of another kind to respond to God in faith, and their response to Jesus at death will always be consistent with their earlier stance toward God.

4. This view is not to be confused with the Catholic doctrine of purgatory. Classically, purgatory refers to a realm in which the souls of believers in Christ are thoroughly "purged" of any remaining sin prior to entering into God's presence. This doctrine does not offer a theory of salvation for those who do not believe in Christ or who have not heard the gospel. Unfortunately, space limitations preclude us from discussing purgatory in this book. For a good Protestant analysis and critique, see Norman L. Geisler and Ralph E. MacKenzie, *Roman Catholics and Protestants: Agreements and Differences* (Grand Rapids: Baker, 1995), 331–55.

5. On the teaching that the Mormon gospel will be preached to the dead, see Robert L. Millet and Joseph Fielding McConkie, *The Life Beyond* (Salt Lake City: Bookcraft, 1986), 36–58; Richard R. Hopkins, *Biblical Mormonism: A Biblical Basis for LDS Theology* (Bountiful, UT: Horizon, 1994), 239–53; and Jay A. Parry and Donald W. Parry, *Understanding Death and the Resurrection* (Salt Lake City: Deseret, 2003), 103–21.

6. Gabriel Fackre, "Divine Perseverance," in *What about Those Who Have Never Heard: Three Views on the Destiny of the Unevangelized*, ed. Gabriel Fackre, Ronald H. Nash, John Sanders (Downers Grove, IL: InterVarsity Press, 1995), 71–95.

7. Tiessen, *Who Can Be Saved?* 32–33, 36–38.

8. E.g., Donald Lake, Evert D. Osburn, and George Goodman, cited in Sanders, *No Other Name?* 168–69.

9. Not everyone who adheres to the idea of God having middle knowledge holds to inclusivism. Notably William Lane Craig, "'No Other Name': A Middle Knowledge Perspective on the Exclusivity of Salvation through Christ," *Faith and Philosophy* 6 (1989): 172–88. Craig argues that God knows who would respond to the gospel if they heard it and makes sure that all such persons do receive a human witness to the gospel. This article and later writings by Craig on the same subject are available *www.leaderu.com/offices/billcraig/menus/particularism.html*.

10. Tiessen's view is best classified as a form of pietistic inclusivism; see his Theses 4–7 in *Who Can Be Saved?* 23–24, and his defense of those theses, 104–64. Tiessen uses the term *accessibilism* for any view, includ-

ing his own, that agrees "that Jesus Christ is exclusively God's means of salvation" but also "that God makes salvation accessible to people who do not receive the gospel" (33). Tiessen differentiates accessibilism from *religious instrumentalism*, the view (such as held by Karl Rahner or Hans Küng) that God intentionally uses other religions to save some people. We indirectly critiqued religious instrumentalism in the previous chapter and will not be discussing it here.

11. Tiessen cites John R. W. Stott, J. I. Packer, and others who express agnosticism about those who have not heard the gospel (ibid., 38–40). For a recent article from this perspective, see R. Todd Mangum, "Is There a Reformed Way to Get the Benefits of the Atonement to 'Those Who Have Never Heard'?" *JETS* 47 (2004): 121–36.

12. Ronald H. Nash, *When a Baby Dies: Answers to Comfort Grieving Parents* (Grand Rapids: Zondervan, 1999), 98.

13. Ronald H. Nash, "Restrictivism," in *What about Those Who Have Never Heard?* 115–16; also *Is Jesus the Only Savior?* (Grand Rapids: Zondervan, 1994), 127. See also Robert L. Reymond, "The 'Very Pernicious and Detestable' Doctrine of Inclusivism," online article: *www.knox seminary.org/Prospective/Faculty/KnoxPulpit/rreymond_perniciousdoctrine.html.*

14. See F. Duane Lindsey, *The Servant Songs: A Study in Isaiah* (Chicago: Moody Press, 1985); see also the chapters on Isaiah in Gerard Van Groningen, *Messianic Revelation in the Old Testament* (Grand Rapids: Baker, 1990).

15. R. Bryan Widbin, "Salvation for People Outside Israel's Covenant?" in *Through No Fault of Their Own: The Fate of Those Who Have Never Heard,* ed. William V. Crockett and James G. Sigountos (Grand Rapids: Baker, 1991), 81.

16. See especially Nash, *When a Baby Dies,* 59–70, and others whom he cites. Also reaching the same conclusion is Millard J. Erickson, *How Shall They Be Saved? The Destiny of Those Who Do Not Hear about Jesus* (Grand Rapids: Baker, 1996), 235–53.

17. David K. Clark, "Warfield, Infant Salvation, and the Logic of Calvinism," *JETS* 27 (1984); Sanders, *No Other Name?* 287–305; Tiessen, *Who Can Be Saved?* 204–16.

18. John F. MacArthur, "The Salvation of Babies Who Die, Part 1," sermon, Grace Community Church, Sun Valley, Calif., see *www.ondoctrine.com/2mac0142.htm.*

19. Sanders, *No Other Name?* 303; Tiessen, *Who Can Be Saved?* 212. The reference to "sentimental reasons" comes from Clark, "Warfield, Infant Salvation," 462.

Chapter 15: No Heaven for the Heathen?

1. Cf. Tiessen, *Who Can Be Saved?* 116–19.
2. Although our focus here is on the salvation of those who have no access to the revelations given to the world through the Jews, we are not denying that Jews also need to hear the gospel.
3. Tiessen, *Who Can Be Saved?* 216–25 (quote on 218).
4. Ibid., 219–20.
5. See Douglas Moo, "Romans 2: Saved Apart from the Gospel?" in *Through No Fault of Their Own*, ed. Crockett and Sigountos, 137–45.
6. Every translation of this controversial passage makes certain interpretive decisions, especially in 3:18–19 and 4:6. We recommend reading the passage in two or three versions to see some of the translation issues.
7. See John H. Elliott, *1 Peter: A New Introduction and Commentary* (AB 37B; New York: Doubleday, 2000), 730–35.
8. In view of the use of the same term "the dead" in verse 5, this explanation fits the context better than the view that Peter is referring to those who had been dead spiritually before hearing the gospel.
9. For defenses of this view (that Christ preached repentance through Noah), see Wayne Grudem, "Christ Preaching through Noah: 1 Peter 3:19–20 in the Light of Dominant Themes in Jewish Literature," *TrinJ* NS 7 (1986): 3–31; John S. Feinberg, "1 Peter 3:18–20, Ancient Mythology, and the Intermediate State," *WTJ* 48 (1986): 303–36; Erickson, *How Shall They Be Saved?* 165–73.
10. The classic work advancing this view (that Christ proclaimed victory over fallen angelic spirits) is W. J. Dalton, *Christ's Proclamation to the Spirits: A Study of 1 Peter 3:18–4:6* (AnBib 23, rev. ed.; Rome: Pontifical Biblical Institute, 1989 [originally 1965]). For recent defenses, see Elliott, *1 Peter*, 637–710; Karen H. Jobes, *1 Peter* (BECNT; Grand Rapids: Baker, 2005), 235–60.
11. Packer, "Evangelicals and the Way of Salvation," in *Evangelical Affirmations*, 123.

Chapter 16: Movin' on Up!

1. This is a very abbreviated description of the three kingdoms; see Bowman, "Latter-day Saints," 90–91, and the sources cited there, for more precise explanations. In particular, note that Mormons believe that there are three heavens, or "degrees of glory," within the "celestial kingdom."
2. *NET Bible*, comments on 2 Cor. 12:2, online at *www.bible.org/net bible2/index.php?header=&book=2co&chapter=12*.

3. *Worship the Only True God* (Brooklyn: Watchtower Bible & Tract Society, 2002), 120–27.

4. "The Other Sheep and the Lord's Evening Meal," *Watchtower* (Feb. 15, 1985), 15–21.

5. "The Other Sheep and the New Covenant," *Watchtower* (Feb. 1, 1998), 18–19.

6. *Pay Attention to Daniel's Prophecy!* (Brooklyn: Watchtower Bible & Tract Society, 1999), 286–93. Between 1948 and 1984, only 292 persons were recognized as new members of the anointed class; "Must All True Christians Be Ministers?" *Watchtower* (Aug. 15, 1984), 13–14.

7. See further Robert M. Bowman Jr., *Jehovah's Witnesses* (Zondervan Guide to Cults and Religious Movements; Grand Rapids: Zondervan, 1995), 48–59.

Chapter 17: When Heaven and Earth Shall Be One

1. Randy Alcorn, *Heaven* (Wheaton, IL: Tyndale, 2004), 58.

2. We are not here addressing questions pertaining to the details of the events associated with Christ's second coming (notably the Rapture and its timing in comparison to Christ's coming and a preceding Great Tribulation).

3. We realize that a question we have not addressed here is the timing and nature of the Millennium and its relation to the Consummation. In broad terms, the view we are presenting on the New Heavens and New Earth is consistent with any of the major Christian views on the Millennium (premillennial, amillennial, and postmillennial).

4. Alcorn, *Heaven*, 58.

5. Ibid., 472.

6. We are referring here to differences in hermeneutical approaches, not to differences over the Millennium. Interpreters of very different approaches to the literal/symbolic dynamic in Revelation can and do share the same millennial perspective.

7. Vern S. Poythress, "Genre and Hermeneutics in Rev 20:1–6," *JETS* 36 (1993): 41–54.

8. William R. Newell, *The Book of the Revelation* (Chicago: Moody Press, 1935), 348.

9. Alcorn, *Heaven*, 241.

10. Ibid., 475.

11. See Robert H. Gundry, "The New Jerusalem People as Place, not Place for People," *NovT* 29 (1987): 254–64.

12. C. S. Lewis, *Mere Christianity* (New York: Macmillan, 1960), 121, quoted in Martindale, *Beyond the Shadowlands*, 40.

13. The orthodox Christian doctrine of creation holds that the universe was made "out of nothing," meaning that God called it into existence without using preexisting, eternal materials. For a recent defense of this doctrine, see Paul Copan and William Lane Craig, *Creation out of Nothing: A Biblical, Philosophical, and Scientific Exploration* (Grand Rapids: Baker, 2004).

14. For these arguments, see, for example, Pilchan Lee, *The New Jerusalem in the Book of Revelation* (WUNT 2/129; Tübingen: Mohr Siebeck, 2001), 268.

15. Ben Witherington III, *Revelation* (NCBC; Cambridge, UK, and New York: Cambridge Univ. Press, 2003), 254 (on Rev. 21:2).

16. So also Alcorn, *Heaven*, xx.

SCRIPTURE INDEX

Please note that boldface numbers indicate where
major discussions of the particular verses take place.

ABOUT THE AUTHORS

Kenneth D. Boa (PhD, New York University; DPhil, University of Oxford) is the president of Reflections Ministries and of Trinity House Publishers. His recent publications include *Conformed to His Image*, *Living What You Believe*, and *Sacred Readings*. You can find his ministry online at kenboa.org.

Robert M. Bowman Jr. is the manager of apologetics and interfaith evangelism for the North American Mission Board (4truth.net). His recent publications include *Putting Jesus in His Place: The Case for the Deity of Christ*. He coauthored two Gold Medallion books with Ken Boa, *An Unchanging Faith in a Changing World* and *Faith Has Its Reasons*. You can also find him online at biblicalapologetics.net.

We want to hear from you. Please send your comments about this book to us in care of zreview@zondervan.com. Thank you.